PROJECTS KEPT S
IN 90 MINUTE

T!
You r

17/7₁

I2252150

For a complete list of Management Books 2000 titles
visit our web-site on http://www.mb2000.com

Other titles in the 'in Ninety Minutes' series are:

25 Management Techniques in 90 Minutes
5S Kaizen in 90 Minutes
Active Learning in 90 Minutes
Become a Meeting Anarchist in 90 Minutes
Budgeting in 90 Minutes
Building a Website Using a CMS in 90 Minutes
Credit Control in 90 Minutes
Damn Clients! in 90 Minutes
Deal With Debt in 90 Minutes
Difficult Decisions Solved in 90 Minutes
Effective Media Coverage in 90 Minutes
Emotional Intelligence in 90 Minutes
Faster Promotion in 90 Minutes
Find That Job in 90 Minutes
Funny Business in 90 Minutes
Getting More Visitors to Your Website in 90 Minutes
Learn to Use a PC in 90 Minutes
Networking in 90 Minutes
Payroll in 90 Minutes
Perfect CVs in 90 Minutes
Plan a New Website in 90 Minutes
Practical Negotiating in 90 Minutes
Run a Successful Conference in 90 Minutes
Selling Advertising space in 90 Minutes
Strengths Coaching in 90 Minutes
Supply Chain in 90 Minutes
Telling People in 90 Minutes
Understand Accounts in 90 Minutes
Working Together in 90 Minutes

PROJECTS KEPT SIMPLE

in 90 Minutes

Mike Watson

2000

SANDWELL LIBRARY & INFORMATION SERVICE	
I2252150	
Bertrams	10/07/2009
658.404	£9.99
OL	

Copyright © Mike Watson 2009

All rights reserved. No part of this publication may be reproduced, stored in a retrieval system, or transmitted in any form or by any means, electronic, mechanical, photocopying, recording, or otherwise without the prior permission of the publishers.

First published in 2009 by Management Books 2000 Ltd
Forge House, Limes Road
Kemble, Cirencester
Gloucestershire, GL7 6AD, UK
Tel: 0044 (0) 1285 771441
Fax: 0044 (0) 1285 771055
Email: info@mb2000.com
Web: www.mb2000.com

This book is sold subject to the condition that it shall not, by way of trade or otherwise, be lent, resold, hired out, or otherwise circulated without the publisher's prior consent in any form of binding or cover other than that in which it is published and without a similar condition including this condition being imposed upon the subsequent purchaser.

British Library Cataloguing in Publication Data is available

ISBN 9781852526122

Contents

Part 1

Introduction

1

Introduction

How lucky you would be...

Imagine how lucky you would be if you were appointed to be the project manager of the next Olympic Games!

The last few Olympic Games have been held up as examples of excellent project management, and rightly so, but being the project manager for such events is easy.

For example, the budget for just the project management for an Olympic Games runs into millions of dollars. There will be a project support team numbering more than 100 people, for years and years. The project manager will never have to pick up a paint brush or a spade. People would expect the project to be managed properly, and will be willing to provide the budget and support network to make sure it will be a success.

How unlucky you are...

Imagine just how unlucky you actually are. You call in at your office kitchen on your way to your desk, and start to make a cup of coffee. The boss walks past, and hands you a piece of paper. The boss says 'This has just arrived – have a look at it will you, and work out what we should do about it.'

Note: at no time in the conversation does the boss use the words 'project' or 'project manager'. The task is probably too small to be considered 'officially' as a project. It might only be a few days work, spread out over the few weeks, fitting in alongside your other day-to-day commitments.

Why did the boss give this to you? Well, it falls into your area of interest and expertise. You would be a little upset if the boss had given it to someone else. By the time you've read the document the boss has gone. Your coffee is ready, so you go back to your desk, sit down, and think about the task.

You are now at a potentially dangerous moment. What you do next is going to have a massive influence on the chances of this piece of work being successful.

What many of us do is to think along these lines (usually unconsciously, not thought out at all):

- You know what has to be done and you have a pretty good idea of how to do it.
- You find the task interesting.
- Time is tight.
- You certainly don't want to waste precious time messing about with fancy project management stuff.
- You've not been trained in project management.
- It's not actually a project, is it?
- You don't have any project management software installed on your PC.

You jump straight in. After all, you've got the email, or minutes of a meeting, or letter from a customer, or whatever it was from the boss in your hand.

You apply yourself to the work, using all your technical skills, knowledge and experience, in the most professional manner.

You do an excellent job.

But sometimes, even whilst you are working on it, you have the nagging feeling that maybe you could be controlling things a bit better.

The implications of this approach are:

- **You have no plan** – so when you are asked if it is going well you have to say 'yes'.

- **You are never sure if it will be finished on time** – so you just have to work through your lunch breaks, early mornings and late nights just to stay on top.
- **When the boss asks** 'can you just do this as well?,' you have to say yes, as you have no idea of the potential effect
- **You can't involve anyone else.** Because you have no clear idea what to do yourself, you cannot delegate
- **When it starts to slip,** you make the macho decision to really go for it.
- **When you finish it, and had it over,** you are furious with yourself, because the boss says 'yes, it's good but it is not exactly what I meant.'
- **And now other work has to slip while you do this job all over again, trying to get it right this time.**

From the moment you make the decision to jump straight in, the project is out of control. You will be pulled around by outside influences and you will have no means of managing changes, measuring progress and checking quality. You will doubtless do an excellent technical job but it may well be the wrong one.

So, if you recognise yourself here, then this book and the practical approaches described in it are for you.

Do you undertake projects?

If you undertake items of work that

- create something new, beyond routine operations
- fulfil some measurable business objectives
- consume company resources

then you are probably running projects. Many of us run projects without even knowing it, or without looking for tools and techniques from the project management toolkit to help us survive the experience.

When you run large projects you will probably use your organisation's standard, formalised approach to project management.

But what methodology do you use for the smaller projects, the 'can you just do this' pieces of work that creep under the radar?

This book is for people in both categories; those of us who don't run formal projects but who carry out assignments for the boss, and those of us who use formal methodologies for certain types of project but who are looking for a lightweight approach to the smaller, lower risk projects.

What will the book cover?

'Project Management' is not a 'one size fits all' set of recipes; 'just do this and all will be well' does NOT apply here. Every project is different, and a fixed standard approach will mislead people into thinking that managing projects is simply a matter of following the rules in the textbook.

What we have here is a process-based approach to project management, in that the book follows the steps you would typically go through in running a project. However, where the methodology outlined in this book differs from most other methodologies is that it encourages the project manager to be very selective about the bureaucracy. Yes, there has to be some documentation, but let's keep it simple and appropriate.

The starting point for the methodology is 'if you could run your project quite safely and successfully on the back of an envelope why would you do anything else?'

Under some circumstances it may be necessary to add an extra envelope, but only if you, the project manager, think it is going to be of benefit to you.

The methodology described and explained in this book is called PKS, Projects Kept Simple. The methodology includes process descriptions and a few sample forms – all you need to manage a range of projects.

As you progress through the book you will see how the various forms can be used to support your project management. The forms are NOT covered by the copyright arrangements for the book. Please feel free to copy them, alter them and use them to make your life a little easier.

The book uses a case study to illustrate the techniques described. The case study is a very simple project, designed so that you can see project management in action.

Finally, just in case your small project turns out to be a large project in disguise, there is a chapter called 'And Now for the Big Time'. This gives an overview of some of the project management techniques used on larger projects.

2

The Case Study

The Background

Park House is a fine country house set in 200 hectares of the finest English countryside. The house can be traced back 300 years, and has been extensively refurbished whilst staying in tune with its environment. Most of the land has now been sold off for farming and rural development.

The house is owned by a small local company, who have redeveloped Park House into a management training centre, with bedroom, catering and training facilities for 40 students. For all day-to-day decisions there is a management committee made up of representatives of several of the small training companies that use it.

PKS Training Limited uses the house and grounds as a base for their operations. The company runs residential courses (about 3 per month) at Park House.

Of particular interest are the splendid gardens, which contain a selection of magnificent mature shrubs set amongst well-tended lawns leading down to a lake. The lake is stocked with very rare freshwater fish and plants, and both the lake and its banks have been declared a nature reserve.

Over the last few weeks, however, several fish have been seen floating on the surface of the lake. Some of the water plants are also showing signs of distress.

As a member of the management committee, Mike Watson from PKS Training has called in the local environmentalist retained as a consultant by Park House.

The environmentalist, Herb Erriott, has established that the lake is suffering from biological contamination (from raw sewage), and that action must be taken promptly to discover and deal with the cause of the contamination. He has stated that if the situation is not rectified within two weeks the entire lake will be dead.

Unfortunately, the Wildlife Trust (a local environmental pressure group) have heard about the problem, and want to know what Park House is going to do to safeguard this important and valuable local natural amenity. The Wildlife Trust is prepared to go to court, if necessary, to stop all use of Park House until the problem is solved. They are waiting to see how we plan to repair the leaking pipe and restore the environment to something suitable for fish and plants.

A brief examination of the plans for the site show that the main drain from the house runs under the lake on its way out to the main drain in the road.

Mike Watson decides to call in the local drainage experts, a well-respected engineering company called Bodgitt and Duck. This firm carries out an extensive survey, and discovers the following:

- The pipe down to the lake from the house and training centre is fine.
- The pipe from its exit from the lake down to the main road is fine.
- There is a leak under the lake (identified by means of a dye test down the pipe).

Mike Watson asks Bodgitt and Duck (B&D) to investigate possible ways of fixing the pipe. B&D carry out their investigation and report as follow:

- They have tried inserting a liner through the pipe, but this failed because of the way that the pipe is damaged. This also explains why the lake is not draining out of the pipe, but sewage is leaking into the lake. This also explains how the damage was sustained. Two weeks ago one of the other training companies ran a management training event that involved the construction of rafts in the lake. Somewhere during this event the pipe suffered damage.
- Installing a completely new pipe around the lake has been rejected by the Wildlife Trust, as this would cause extensive

18

damage to the banks of the lake, which are important nesting areas and refuges for some rare mammals, reptile and birds.

- A better long-term solution would be to replace the broken section of pipe. Technically this would be simple, even though B&D rule out building temporary dams around the leaking pipe (too risky – may cause even more damage to the pipe).
- B&D state that it would be easy to drain the entire lake (this is not a big lake), replace the pipe, and refill the lake with clean water from the local mains supply.

Mike Watson asks Herb Erriott if this could be feasible from an environmental point of view, and Herb is sure that this method of approach is sensible. He says that the fish can be caught and stored in a large tank for several days without problems. The plants are more difficult. These are very rare aquatic plants. They cannot be uprooted or exposed to the air. Herb says that if we cover the plants during the draining of the lake (whilst the level of water in the lake is reducing), then they will survive for 48 hours. B&D confirm that the technical work in replacing the broken section of pipe will take no more than 6 hours, so it seems that we have a solution.

There is one huge business constraint hanging over this repair job. Park House is fully booked for a variety of events for the next 6 weeks. All of the companies that use Park House are small to medium-sized training companies, who charge premium rates for managers to attend Park House. If the facility has to close for the work to be carried out then more than one of these small companies will lose revenue, possibly to the point of financial difficulties.

In fact, if the courses have to be taken away to hotels the training companies will have to bear this additional cost themselves; there is no insurance cover for this eventuality.

There is one possibility. All of the courses are finished by 14:00 on Friday afternoon, and Park House remains empty over every weekend. Delegates begin to arrive at 09:00 on Monday morning, so the job could be carried out over a weekend. Many of the courses end in examinations, so there cannot be any noise before 14:00 (for example the running of pumps to drain the lake will be too noisy), but certainly the site and the project team could be prepared ready for a start at 14:00.

Mike Watson has been asked by the other training companies to act as a single point of contact for the project (the sponsor), and has been delegated a budget for the project.

Let us assume that you are a project management expert, a trainer working for PKS Training Ltd, and have been asked to manage this project to a successful conclusion.

3

An Overview of the Projects Kept Simple Process

A project follows a lifecycle, starting with the beginning and ending at the end. Of course, project management being, as it is, a branch of general management, we cannot use terms as prosaic as 'beginning' and 'end'.

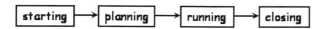

In generic terms, then, a project follows these 'phases'. It is instructive to realise that a significant amount of project management activity is carried out before the project as such seems to get under way.

The reasons for this are important, and set the theme for much of what 'project management' is about:

- Before we start any real work we must agree what it is that we are trying to do, why we are trying to do it (usually from a business point of view), and what the success criteria are.
- We should get a clear understanding of the way forward before we start.
- If we are going to have argument and disagreement about the project it is best to have this at the start (the cheap end of the project) rather than at the end (the expensive end).
- If there are areas of uncertainty these should be identified and understood at the start.

If we can have discussions about these project parameters at the beginning, then, if we have disagreement, it will be easier to amend the project. If we have the discussion at the end, when we have delivered the wrong thing, we (the organisation) are stuck with a failed project.

What happens in each phase?

Every project passes through these phases. A very small project may pass through Startup and Planning within a matter of minutes, whereas the Startup for an Olympic Games project may take months, and involve dozens of people.

Project Startup

There are three main processes within project startup, as follows:

- Project Definition: getting agreement to WHAT it is we are trying to do, and WHY. We are definitely not making commitments about the HOW.
- Roles and Responsibilities: identifying the key players, and setting out their responsibilities.
- Managing Stakeholders: identifying the other players in the project, and starting to think about what they want, and where they might be coming from.

Project Planning

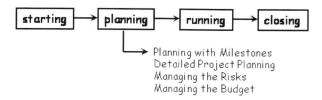

There are four processes within project planning, as follows:

- Planning with Milestones: establishing a structure or framework for the project, by identifying key decision points linked to the production of major deliverables.
- Detailed Project Planning: sorting out the detail of who will do what, how and when.
- Managing the Risks: enhancing the robustness of the project plan, by planning to manage risks in advance.
- Managing the Budget: identifying where the money will be spent.

Running the Project

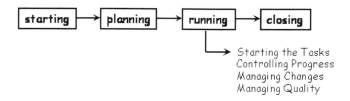

There are four processes involved in running the project, as follows:

- Starting the Tasks: making sure that tasks actually start when you want them to start.
- Controlling Progress: measuring progress, taking corrective actions, reporting progress.
- Managing Changes: dealing with the inevitable requests for change in an orderly manner.
- Managing Quality: making sure that the project delivers quality end and component products.

Closing the Project

There are two processes within project closure, as follows:

- Closing the Project: making sure that the customer is happy with the end result, dealing with outstanding issues, and closing the files.
- Learning to Improve: taking a constructive look back at the way you managed the project, in order to get it better next time.

Why follow such a process?

These processes outlines above might seem like a lot of long-winded bureaucracy, but put yourself in the shoes of your project sponsor (probably the person who will pay for the project, but certainly the person who wants the outcome). If the sponsor asks you how you are planning to run the project, your reply should NOT be one of the following:

- 'Well, I'm going to make it up as I go along, as I find that this is a much more flexible and exciting way to do it.'
- 'Well, I'm not really sure.'
- 'Let's just wait and see what happens, shall we?'
- 'I don't like the company standard methodology, so I'm going to use common sense.'

Not only does a well thought-out structure approach help the sponsor (in underlining your credibility, and so on), but it will also help you. Why on earth would you wish to reinvent the wheel, when you can use an approach that has been used successfully many times?

Summary

The fool learns from his mistakes; the wise man learns from the mistakes of others. Tap into a rich vein of project management expertise by following an approach that has a great track record on a wide range of project types.

Part 2

Starting Well

$$4$$

Project Definition

Where are we?

Well, obviously we are near the beginning of the project, but it is worthwhile remembering what comes next: after definition comes planning, NOT the project. This means that the Project Definition Phase is not a huge decision point on the project. It simply allows the project manager to understand the project a little more, in order to carry out some detailed planning. The big decision comes after the planning is complete, as by that stage all the key players will have a much better understanding of how the project will run.

The project definition phase for an Olympic Games project would take months, and involve many high-powered resources. The output from such a phase would be legal document describing the project, its deliverables, all the key roles, control mechanisms, risk and issue management systems, and so on. The project team would be foolish in the extreme to start the project without going through this complex definition phase, which would probably be treated as a project in its own right.

For a smaller projects we might be talking about just a few days (for a 3 month project), or 10 minutes (for a 3 day project). In all cases, however, the vital few items to understand, document and agree are the same.

Many project managers make the mistake of trying to understand everything at this early stage in the project's lifecycle. This is not only unnecessary but also dangerous. The more detail we have now, especially about our proposed method of approach, the more we might be tying our hands together, limiting our options, when this is not required.

Figure PD01 shows the way in which the vital information about a project is identified and documented in a particular sequence. It is most important to understand the WHAT and WHY (and obtain agreement that your understanding is correct) before you waste any time planning what might be the wrong thing.

The What, Why, How, Who and When

	Phase	technical term
What	Definition	Scope
Why	Definition	Objectives
How	Planning	Schedule
Who	Planning	Schedule
When	Planning	Schedule

Figure PD01

It can be very embarrassing to have to retract a plan issued too early. It starts to erode your credibility. So, sort out the WHAT and WHY first, and then do the planning which will sort out the HOW, WHO and WHEN.

Date-Driven Projects

Of course your sponsor may have already told you the When. Actually, the sponsor may have already told everybody else the When as well! Target dates are often identified and published before the project really starts to take shape. There may be excellent reasons for this. Maybe the law is changing on a particular date, and without your new website changes, or HR processes, or whatever, the organisation will be in trouble. No amount of complaining on your part can alter the fact that sometimes the target date is outside your control, and you have to use your skills to deliver by that date. Just make sure that you discover this commitment during the project definition!

Project Management Law number 1: The Sponsor knows nothing...

It is always useful to consider why a sponsor (your boss, for example) asks you to run a project on his/her behalf.

If we set aside any devious or machiavellian reasons, there are only two possible reasons:

- The sponsor could run the project themselves – they have the skills and technical knowledge – but they do not have the time, so you are being asked to do the detailed work on the sponsor's behalf.
- The sponsor does not have the skills or technical knowledge to run the project, so you are being asked to exercise your skills to run the project.

In both of these cases you should be aware that you are being asked to do two things. Obviously you are being asked to deliver the desired outcome of the project, but, equally importantly, you are being asked to do the second-level thinking for the sponsor (remember, he or she either hasn't got the time or the knowledge to do this thinking for themselves). The role title you are taking on is 'project manager', not 'project slave'.

This means that you must assume that whatever the sponsor tells you should NOT be accepted blindly, but thought about, tested, validated, challenged. If you find that one of the things the sponsor wants you to deliver just cannot be done, then the quicker you identify this, and go back to the sponsor with some viable and effective alternatives, the better.

If you assume that 'the sponsor knows nothing', this will be a safe attitude for you to take. Obviously this is not meant to be rude, but a good defence mechanism for the project manager.

For example, the Lake project sponsor may set as a constraint that there should be no further loss of fish or plants (to show that the job is being carried out in a responsible manner). Well, we know that some fish and plants are dying now – that's how the project started in the first place – so some of them must be very sick right now. However good a job you do some will die, and it is unreasonable for the sponsor to set this unattainable target for your performance. It will be far better to ask the environmental expert to set some targets based upon his superior technical knowledge.

Every project has two ends: a cheap end and a very expensive end. Asking questions at the cheap end may feel cheeky and dangerous, but try asking them at the expensive end!

Some Questions to Ask

Start the process of project definition by asking questions. You may have been given something in writing to start the ball rolling, but it is essential that you start to think not just about the immediate project but also the surrounding business environment. You may be able to go back to the sponsor to ask these questions; failing this, try to find the answers yourself. The answers will be very useful in helping you to decide how to approach the project. If you ask a question and cannot get an answer this is also very valuable; it shows that there is a risk in the project, caused by some key factors being unknown at the outset. Not asking the questions will be your first mistake; many more will follow as a result of your going into the unknown.

There are 11 groups of questions, with subsidiary questions in each group, as follows:

- **Time Constraints**
  Is there an end date? Is it fixed? Who fixed it? How fixed is it? Is there a constraint on the start date? Are there intermediate dates

that must be met in some way? Are the constraints on the availability of key personnel? Is it month, quarter or year end?

- **Project Profile**

Is the reputation of the company, division, management team or yourself at stake? Is there likely to be ongoing high-level or external interest in the project? Will the project be accompanied by publicity?

- **Costs and Benefits**

Has a Cost/Benefit Analysis been carried out? How long ago? By whom? On what basis? Do you have to stick to it? What assumptions were made? Are the costs constrained or prioritised?

- **Business Risk**

How badly will the organisation suffer if the project fails, or the final end product does not perform as well as hoped? Will there be a knock-on effect elsewhere if it fails?

- **Project Scope**

How many business functions are involved? What has been left out? Has this been agreed? Which locations are involved? How will this project interface with other projects, and what plans exist for those projects?

- **Background**

Is this a new business area, or the first time that the project team has come into contact with the business area? Have you done anything similar in the past? What happened? Are you taking over something that has already started? Why? Are the key players up to speed with the project?

- **Requirements**

Is the customer clearly identified? Is the customer different from the end user of the project deliverables? Are the requirements likely to be well-known, understood and constant during the project? Will the requirements have to be flexible? Is the customer prepared to commit to the requirements?

- **Involvement**

Is there commitment at high level? How does this manifest itself? Are the key management players aware of the potential size of their commitment?

- **Technology**

Is the technology in place right now? Will it be installed during the project? When, in relation to the project? Has it been ordered? Is there any fallback? Is a specification available? How many suppliers are involved? Who is responsible for connecting the components together? Is the technology new to the eventual end user, or the project team? How reliable must it be? Can reliability be established before operational use?

- **Resources**

Is it possible to identify what disciplines are needed, when and how many? Are the skills available in-house? Contractors? Out-sourcing? What training is needed for this project? How likely is it that resources will be made available? Are these resources aware of the project? Will they be full-time or part-time? What other commitments will they have? What are the relative priorities? Who will resolve disputes or prioritisation? Who will have management authority over them?

- **Project Management**

How will the project be managed? What support might be available to the project manager? What standards and quality processes are in place? Are these understood and used by the project team?

Using the Answers

Having established the answers to these questions you can now begin to understand the shape of the project.

For example, if you discover that the target is absolutely fixed for legal reasons then you might consider adding some contingency plans into the project, whereby you create a standby solution as well as the main project outcome, just in case you are delayed.

For example, you may discover that certain technology will not be fully available for your project. By realising this at an early stage you may have enough time to investigate alternative technical solutions that do not rely on the suspect technology.

On the Lake case study project you may discover that no-one has any real idea how many fish there are in the lake, and how well they might survive the draining and refilling operation. It may be a good idea to commission Herb Erriott (the environmental scientist) to carry out a detailed survey before you start, just to set some baselines.

Starting the Project Definition

Once you have the answers (or, indeed, no answers) you can start to draft the Project Definition. Note the word 'draft'. You can only ever draft this definition; it will never be final until the sponsor has accepted it. This is also a guide as to how to produce this draft document – talk to the sponsor as often as possible throughout this brief process.

Form PKS01, in the Appendices to this book, is the PKS Project Definition form. It uses both sides of one page of A4 paper, but, for many projects, it is all you need to manage the project safely and successfully. The PKS methodology really does try to keep the bureaucracy to a minimum.

There is one other document that you should be creating and maintaining right from the start of the project definition, and that is the assumptions list. This does not have to be very formal in its layout, but it is a vital part of your project management plan. There is no sample form in the appendix for the assumptions list. Most people start a simple spreadsheet as soon as they start working on the definition, and keep this updated as the project unfurls. The uses of such a list are described at the end of this chapter.

We will examine each part of the project definition in turn.

Project Objectives

These correspond to the 'Why' we are doing this. There may be several objectives, and, if the sponsor is on the ball, they may be prioritised.

Objectives should be written in business terms, and set out what we are trying to achieve with this project. They are NOT a shopping list of all the things we are going to do during it, but more the reasons why we are doing them.

These are the objectives of the project, not objectives for how successfully the business will use whatever the project will deliver.

For example, if your project is to create a new meetings room booking system that will save £10,000 every year for 5 years you cannot be held responsible for the delivery of savings of £50,000 over 5 years. You will not be running the bookings system, so the achievement of the business benefit will be beyond your influence or control. It will take 5 years after your project has ended to prove this benefit. This is not part of your project, but it is the ongoing business responsibility of the sponsor. He or she will need to be satisfied that at the handover of the new bookings system you have created the capability to save £10,000 per year for 5 years. You must be able to prove this as part of the project closure.

Project Objectives should state measurable targets for what is to be delivered, based upon business benefit. Here is another example. Let us say that your project is to introduce a new training record form for your department. If the objectives are stated as 'to introduce a new training record form for the department', then almost any form will do, even if it causes nothing but trouble for the department staff.

You need to know what the underlying reasons are for introducing this form; these reasons will help you agree on the business objectives. These might be: to eliminate duplication in the department's training and development planning by implementing a system to record up-to-date and accurate information about staff training.

OK, so this new objective is longer than the first attempt, but it links your project to the wider business objective of improving resource development and planning. Your project must now deliver a system that allows up-to-date recording of training, which might be translated as 'capable of capturing training information no more than 4 weeks after a training event'. This, in turn, will drive the design for collecting training data, and so on. The project objectives not only give you a target to aim at but will also help to direct the design of the solution.

Your objectives should focus on what the sponsor hopes to achieve as a result of your project. This probably means that you cannot write the objectives without discussing them with the sponsor. You may also ask the sponsor to prioritise the objectives, but some sponsors are reluctant to do this until the planning phase has begun. They want you to try for it all, and will only discuss compromise and reduced delivery when you can show, by your planning, that you can't deliver it all.

Objectives should be written so that they describe an impact that the project will make, linked to what the project will deliver. The more measurable we can make the objectives the better.

The objectives for the Lake Project are interesting to consider. We should ask ourselves: Why is the sponsor spending money on this right now? Just how much does the sponsor actually care about the fish and plants? I believe that the objectives for the Lake Project are along these lines:

- *To remove the current threat posed by the Wildlife Trust by:*
  - *repairing the pipe so that the pipe passes the test specified in ISO1234;*
  - *restoring the water quality in the lake to the standard defined in ISO9876*

Obviously I have made up these two ISO standards, but the point is that the objectives state several important things:

- *We now know exactly why we are being asked to run this project – this knowledge may be vital later in the project.*
- *We know what standard of work we have to work to.*

36

- *We can see how we can involve two independent experts in proving that we have achieved our objectives.*

It may comes as surprise that these objectives are short. Further detail will come in the Scope and Constraints sections.

Project Scope

This is an outline of what you will have to do to achieve the objectives. The list does not have to be detailed; in fact, if we make the list too detailed we may be confusing people, as it will begin to look like a plan and we haven't done any planning yet.

It is also very useful to list those things which you are NOT going to do, in the form of 'Excluded from Scope'. It is always better to disappoint people at the Project Definition stage (the cheap end) than to find out at the project closure that they had been expecting something from the project that you never meant to deliver.

Scope can be expressed geographically (e.g. the project will address meeting room bookings in the Manchester Office), functionally (e.g. this project will only cover meetings rooms booked by Finance Department), or related to business processes (e.g. this project will not link the meetings rooms booking system to the Automated Catering System).

In many projects the scope may consist of technical drawings and specifications of what is to be produced.

The Scope for the Lake Project may be:

- *Included in Scope:*
  - *Repairing the leak identified in the pipe under the lake (i.e. NOT leaks elsewhere)*
  - *All aspects of fish and plants welfare (even though this may be delegated to the environmental expert, it is still part of the project and ultimately is the project manager's responsibility)*
  - *Restoring the water environment to acceptable standards*

> – *Obtaining relevant permits and permissions associated with disposal of contaminated water and mud*
> – *Managing the sub-contractors*

- *Excluded from the Scope:*
  - *All communications with the media and the Wildlife Trust (agreed that the sponsor will handle this outside of the project)*

So, there should be no surprises at the expensive end of the project. Everyone who reads this will be able to see just what the project consists of, and what it does not contain.

One of the interesting benefits if writing it down like this is that we may have got it completely wrong! The publication of the Project Definition will stimulate a great deal of 'validation' of the project's parameters. It is cheaper to find out now that we have misunderstood our scope than wait until we reach the expensive end.

Constraints

Very few project managers have a completely free hand in the way that they run the project. There are always factors that will affect the way we carry out the job, and these are the project constraints.

The obvious constraints include time, money, materials, availability of team members, rules, standards or processes that must be followed, availability of machinery or other facilities.

The questions you asked at the start of this process will go a long way to helping you identify the constraints. The Constraints section of the Project Definition is your way of proving to the sponsor that you heard all of the things that concern him/her.

The Constraints for the Lake Project are:

- *Time:*
  - *The job must be completed within the next 2 weeks.*

      – *There can be no noise or disruption to the Park House toilets system before 14:00 on Friday, and the works must be complete by 09:00 Monday.*

- *Wildlife:*
  - *The fish can live in a tank for 72 hours without feeding or aeration.*
  - *The plants can survive only if they are covered in black plastic, and then only for a maximum of 48 hours.*

- *Budget:*
  - *There is an initial budget of £15,000.*

Main Deliverables (sometimes called Products)

It can be a good idea to write down and agree the format and purpose (and possibly outline contents) of your final deliverables, and any intermediate deliverables if this will help you.

For example, you may be asked to write a report about the use of business class air travel in your department. Well, anyone can write such a report, but without knowing how it will be used (the purpose) you could spend a lot of time and produce something that is useless. How about: a report into the increasing costs of departmental air travel, with a recommendation about future air travel policy.

Will the report be printed, or will it stay electronic? Is there a company standard for such reports? Will you distribute the whole report, including the detailed notes and analysis of 25 interviews, or will you produce a summary report for general distribution and an appendix to be called for by the enthusiastic few?

It might seem very early to be describing the final product, but the earlier you can get agreement about its quality acceptance criteria the easier it will be for you to plan how to deliver it.

Some deliverables are difficult to see or file at the end of the project, and we must resort to looking for evidence that an acceptable deliverable has been produced.

The real deliverables for the Lake Project are 'A Repaired Pipe' and 'Clean Water'. Well, by the end of the project the pipe will be at the bottom of the lake, so it can't be seen, and although the water may look clean we must sure that the fish and plants agree with us.

So, for the Lake we will have to specify secondary deliverables, as follows:

- *A certificate attesting that the pipe repair has passed ISO1234, signed by Bert Simpson, the foreman of Bodgitt & Duck, Engineers.*
- *A certificate attesting that the water quality meets ISO9876, signed by Herb Erriott, Certified Environmental Consultant.*

These deliverables will be captured by the project manager and placed in the project file, for eventual acceptance by the sponsor at project closure.

External Dependencies

Nowadays, in most organisations, most projects touch other projects, if only through the use of shared resources. Some projects are tightly linked together, almost as two parts of a larger project.

It is most important to understand how your project fits into the wider business environment, both as a sender (you may be producing something that goes on to another project elsewhere, and they are depending on you), and as a receiver (you may be waiting for something from another project, and you will be depending on them).

These links between projects are important. The work you do now during the project definition will set up a communication and control requirement. Managers of linked projects must inform each other if there are delays that will affect a dependant project.

The principal source of dependencies is in shared resources. You may be promised someone to help you, but this will not usually be fulltime. The person will probably have to carry out their day job (the normal things they do from day to day) and fit in your project work alongside it. They may also be assigned to several other projects, not just yours, and it is important for you to be aware of this situation and its potential for problems later. By identifying the situation now and documenting it, you will be starting an early form of risk management.

An external dependency for the Lake Project might be that the wedding party for the daughter of the Chief Executive of PKS Training Ltd will be held on a Saturday during the period of the project, in a large marquee at the side of the Lake! Both you, as the project manager for the Lake Project and the wedding organiser will need to liaise about the weekend works.

An Optional Extra

One other thing to agree at project definition time might be 'tolerance', or just how accurate you need to be when running the project.

For example, if you are running a project with a monthly budget of £10,000 will you have to stop the project if you are £3 over budget at one month end? The answers is probably no. If you can reach agreement on some levels of tolerance with the sponsor, then the project can run in a smoother manner, rather than stop/start.

Tolerance is often expressed in budget terms (e.g. £500 per month, or +/- 5% per month), or time terms (e.g. a milestone can be 5 days delayed). It can be qualified with statements such as 'tolerance of £500 per month will be allowed as long as the project manager can show how the project will be back on track by the next milestone'.

This arrangement can take the pressure off both the project manager and the sponsor.

What is the process?

Don't ask the sponsor to write the project definition! Remember Project Management Law number 1 – the sponsor knows nothing. It is always best if the project manager drafts the definition him/herself.

Obviously listen to the sponsor. Go back to your desk and draft a Project Definition. Take it back for discussion with something like: 'Just in case I didn't fully understand what you asked for I've written it down; please take a look at it will you.' Once you've (both) developed a bit of experience at this, it really won't take long.

You will know that you've cracked it when, the next time the boss wants you to undertake a small project, he/she says: 'But I know that before you start you will draft one of those project definitions and let me have a look at it first.'

Best practice suggests that both parties should sign off this definition. You may not work in an environment where this is the norm; maybe you should start the process of building good habits and best practice in your organisation.

How long will it take?

For a small project (2 weeks to 2 months duration), the drafting of the project definition should take no more than 1 hour. This will be followed with a brief conversation with the sponsor, at which agreement can be reached. So, for the investment of 90 minutes you can feel more confident that you are, at the very least, starting out on the right project.

Assumptions

The very nature of a project is to create something new, something that didn't exist before. This means that all project management and planning activity is speculative, looking into an uncertain future and trying to guess what might happen.

As soon as you start the project definition phase you will enter the realms of fantasy and guesswork. There is nothing wrong with this, as long as you realise that this is where you are.

Make a list of all the assumptions you make, and, where possible, their effects and implications.

For example, you may assume for the Lake Project that there will be enough water to refill the lake in 12 hours. Obviously, if your assumption is incorrect, there is a possibility that it will take longer than 12 hours to refill the lake. Does this matter? Well, at the moment, we cannot tell if it matters or not, so note it down. Later on, when we have a draft project schedule, we can examine our assumptions by using the process of Risk Management.

The assumptions list will form vital input to the detailed project planning, risk management and project control processes.

Make sure that your assumptions are specific and reasonable. For example, an assumption that everything will work according to plan is useless for practical project management purposes.

Some people think that once a Project Definition has been signed off by the sponsor there should not be any assumptions, as the process of discussion and agreement of the definition will have cleared up all of the unknowns. If only this were true. You will find that, when confronted with some of your assumptions, the sponsor will look just as blank as you. Why should the sponsor know any more about the detail of the project than you do? After all, you have been appointed to take care of the details that the sponsor doesn't want to mess with. If you both agree that there are some unknowns in the project and you both accept that the project could start with these unknowns unresolved, then it is safe to start.

Summary

Most projects go wrong because the objectives and scope were poorly understood right from the start, and the project manager, eager to show just what he/she can do, jumped into the project without thinking about it.

Many bosses seem to prefer their project managers to be busy rather than sitting thinking about the project. Secure project definition does not have to take much time, and only a fool would start out on a journey without knowing why or where to end up.

PKS Checklist

Ask the strategic questions	Identify how the answers will shape your project
Agree the Objectives with the sponsor	What the sponsor is trying to achieve with the project; why we are running this project now
Agree the scope	High-level statements of what is included and excluded from the project
Agree the constraints	Time, budget, resources, rules etc
Agree the deliverables	What is to be produced, and how it will be used
Agree the roles and responsibilities	Who is responsible for what
Document the assumptions	And keep this list under review throughout the project

5

Roles and Responsibilities

Where are we?

We are in the project definition phase, trying to understand the roles of the various key players before we make a start on the project.

Every project has at least two key players, namely the sponsor and the project manager. There may be other key players in your project; we will consider the possibilities once we have dealt with the two principal roles.

In simple terms the sponsor is the person who has commissioned the project (the person who wants it carried out) and the project manager is the person who has been delegated the responsibility of carrying it out. It is quite likely that neither of people will have the words 'sponsor' or 'project manager' in their job title, as we are talking about a temporary project role, not a position in the corporate hierarchy.

This difference in the roles means that the sponsor is probably working to a longer horizon than the project manager. Figure RR01 shows how the two roles fit together.

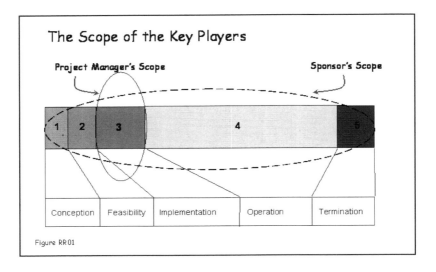

The Scope of the Key Players

Project Manager's Scope

Sponsor's Scope

| 1 | 2 | 3 | 4 | 5 |

| Conception | Feasibility | Implementation | Operation | Termination |

Figure RR01

We can see from RR01 that the informal definition of 'sponsor' given above is not good enough. The better definition is 'the person who wants to achieve business benefit with the project outcome'. This puts the sponsor's role firmly in its place, which is as a representative of the business, who wishes to use the project outcome for a business reason. We can see illustrated in RR01, where the sponsor stays in control of the outcome long after the project manager has delivered it.

In fact many sponsors do not realise that their responsibility is 'to deliver the business benefit' that the project will facilitate. This may take several months (or even years in some cases) to finally achieve.

For many small 'local' projects your sponsor may well be your boss. He or she will ask you to undertake a task, sometimes in a formal manner, sometimes very informally, but he/she is in the role of sponsor for your project.

The role of sponsor carries with it a range of responsibilities, including:

- Set and agree the scope of the project, confirm and authorise stages, obtain necessary resources, monitor and control through the project manager, accept the end product and close the project.

- Delegate the day-to-day project responsibility to the project manager; allow the project manager some agreed tolerances for overruns, etc.
- Use the end product during its operational life; monitor its effectiveness, and achieve the business benefits.

It can be very useful for the long-term success of the project if you spend a few minutes during the project definition phase with the sponsor, making sure that the sponsor understands the role he/she has taken on. This small investment of your time may pay dividends later if you run into problems on the project. You want the sponsor to be on your side, pushing to break the road blocks, acting as a senior management champion for the project. Of course this is more relevant on larger projects that affect much more of the organisation, but the sponsor can be the most useful 'resource' on the project team, and you should try to get the best out of him or her.

Is the Sponsor the Customer?

Well, sometimes but not always. Sometimes the sponsor is a director or manager who represents the business's need, whereas the customer may be the person who will actually use what you deliver.

It can be useful to identify both roles, as you will need to use them differently throughout the project. The sponsor will be making strategic decisions (e.g. shall we cancel this project?), whereas the customer will be involved in more tactical decisions (e.g. what colour will the new walls be painted?).

What is the project manager's role?

This sounds obvious, and can be expressed quite simply as: the project manager must ensure that the project as a whole produces the required end products to the required standard of quality within specified constraints of time and cost.

This is accomplished by the activities of planning, defining objectives and responsibilities, monitoring progress and resource utilisation, taking corrective actions where necessary, and advising the sponsor of status and direction.

There is a further part to the responsibilities of a project manager: the project manager is responsible for making sure that the project produces a result capable of achieving the benefits defined in the business case.

This statement is most important, as it reminds the project manager that the project fits within an overall business environment. It is vital for the project manager to understand this wider environment, even if the project seems so small that it has no need for a formal business case.

It is also vital for the project manager to understand and constantly monitor the objectives, scope and constraints of the project, as they define the project's outcome.

One common difficulty for many project managers is that they are also part of the project team (and, indeed, for many smaller projects the project manager may form 100% of the team!). It can be a matter of concern for the project manager to know precisely which hat (manager or team resource) he or she should be wearing today. We will address this point in more detail in the chapter 'Controlling Progress'.

Other Useful Project Roles

You may require some specific input from key players in your project, and it can be useful to define the responsibility of each key player. There are some generic types of role to consider: auditors, inspectors (e.g. Health & Safety), technical specialists.

There will be roles that are crucial to your project (for example a company auditor who may have to approve something you are proposing in your project).

48

Don't think you have to define the role of every single person in the project. You don't actually know who they all are yet. We are only interested in people who will undertake something unusual for them (and who will therefore appreciate a reminder of what you expect from them) or have a key decision-making role in the project (so they can see the effect they could have).

Presentation

A very effective way of showing how the roles fit together is by means of an organogram (see RR02 for the Lake Project as an example). This is not always appropriate, however, so a simple list of roles, the named individual who has accepted each role, and a line or two outlining the vital aspects of the role from your project's point of view. If you use the PKS forms then there is space on the front of PKS01, Project Definition.

For the Lake Project we might specify the key roles as:

- *Sponsor: Mike Watson; responsible for*
  - *accepting the project definition, project plans, progress reports and project closure report*
  - *allocating the budget to the project*
  - *all aspects of communications with the Wildlife Trust (remember this was ruled out of your scope, as the sponsor wanted to do it himself – a reminder here would be useful)*
- *Project Manager: Jenny Harris; responsible for:*
  - *Blah*
- *Environmental Specialist: Herb Erriott: responsible for:*
  - *Survey to establish numbers of fish and plants*
  - *All aspects of day-to-day fish and plant welfare*
  - *Testing the Lake water after the project, and issuing a certificate to ISO9876*
- *Engineering Supervisor: Bert Simpson: responsible for:*
  - *All aspects of the pipe repair*
  - *Testing the pipe and issuing a certificate to ISO1234*

These two extra roles (Environmental Specialist and Engineering Supervisor) are crucial to your project, as they are the only two roles capable of issuing the certificates that form your major project deliverables. It is prudent to identify and document these roles.

The roles can be shown in an organogram:

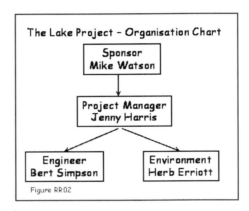

Figure RR02

Even if you use an organogram you should still include the few lines describing the detailed responsibilities.

Summary

'I thought *you* were going to handle that' is a sign of a project that has unclear responsibilities. Sort it out at the beginning, during the project definition phase, and make sure that the project progresses in a controlled manner. If someone is unsure of their ability to deliver their assigned tasks then now is the time to find out, not half way through the project.

6

Managing Stakeholders

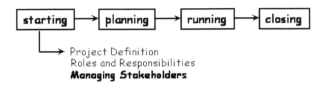

starting → planning → running → closing
Project Definition
Roles and Responsibilities
Managing Stakeholders

Where are we?

We are still in the project definition phase, trying to understand the project and its environment before we make a commitment to start.

Many project managers lose sight of the fact that it is not the project documentation, however excellent it may be, that actually does the work on the project; it is the human beings that do the work. Even at this early stage in the project you should be thinking about the people in the project, and why they should even bother to help you.

This process, thinking about the key players, and trying to get them onto your side, is called stakeholder management.

A stakeholder can be anyone who will be affected by the project (or its outcome), or who can affect the project. Obviously the project sponsor is a key stakeholder (he/she has a strong vested interested in seeing the project through to completion), but there are other less obvious stakeholders who can influence the success of the project, sometimes in a negative way. This means that a stakeholder is anyone who can foul up the project.

The point about identifying them is that you can start the process of building them into the project as allies right from the start, rather than having to recover a poor situation later.

Key players who have been kept well-informed and involved throughout the project are much more likely to act positively when a problem occurs than someone who has been kept in the dark until the bad news breaks.

On many projects the management of stakeholders takes place after the problem has occurred, and often amounts to no more than damage limitation. Of course this is not stakeholder management at all, but a panic reaction towards a group of upset people.

Stakeholder management should be a proactive attempt to get the key players on side, and keep them on side all the way through the project. It is an ongoing process, and must be planned into the project.

On many very large projects skilled professional resources (e.g. Public Relations consultants) would be engaged to focus entirely on this vital aspect of managing the project. On smaller projects it remains the direct responsibility of the project manager.

The process can be split into several parts, as follows:

- Stakeholder identification
- Assessment of potential impact
- Stakeholder Planning
- Stakeholder management actions

We can start these activities now, but we need to keep them under review and revision more or less all the way through the project.

Identifying your Stakeholders

Identifying stakeholders can be an opportunity to involve the project team in part of the project management process. This has benefits for you (a wider spread of knowledge and views about the stakeholders), the team (a feeling of involvement in the project), and the stakeholders (possibly more creative ideas for mobilising them).

By considering all available project documentation a brainstorming activity can be undertaken to identify all those who could affect the project and all those on whom the project could have an effect.

Useful documentation will include:

- the details that started the whole thing off, sometimes called the Project Brief – this may mention people for whom the project is designed to deliver something
- the project definition, as this may mention other key players who must be managed proactively
- any planning documents you may have (actually you may not have anything documented yet – you may have to revisit your stakeholder mobilisation plans later once you have drafted your project plan in a little more detail)

As in all good brainstorming sessions the initial identification should be completely open and unedited, as sometimes stakeholders appear from the most unlikely sources. Don't forget people such as:

- yourself and the project team members
- your boss, and the line managers of any team members
- the sponsor and customer of the project, both at management level and operational level
- 'inspectors' (many projects will contain an element of conforming to rules or regulations, so the regulator or inspector who signs something off for you can affect your project)
- suppliers of goods, services or resources (internal or external)

Assessing their impact

Some stakeholders might have more impact than others, and it is useful to assess your stakeholders in this regard (it will help you to work out a priority system for your actions).

Keep it simple. Use a High/Medium/Low method, and be realistic about the impact that each one could have (it is common to assess too many as High, as we may fear the worst!). Start to build up a Stakeholder Plan (see figure SM01).

Stakeholder Management Plan			
Stakeholder	**impact**	**attitude**	**action**
Figure SH01			

Stakeholder Planning

You must now try to identify just what each stakeholder desires from the project, and what might be their attitude towards the project.

This could be done by brainstorming, by asking other project managers who know the stakeholders, or even by asking the stakeholders directly.

It can be surprising what individual stakeholders actually want. Many bosses, for example, want a quiet life, punctuated by good news. It can be poor management to keep such a boss inundated with news of every penny of expenditure, and every task undertaken.

You might not be able to deliver every desire of every stakeholder, and, indeed, some desires may conflict with the objectives or constraints of the project. However, if this is the case, by never identifying the conflict you may create larger conflicts later in the project.

Also, there may be some desires that despite your best efforts you cannot satisfy. It may be that a team member really wants to try some project management activity during the project, or has asked to be assigned to your project to try out some new technology. In each case you should establish this interest by talking to the individual, and then looking at your project plans for opportunities to satisfy their need. In an ideal world you might be able to satisfy the needs of every individual stakeholder, but this is not always possible.

However, do not despair. If you can demonstrate how

- you have listened to and taken notice of their points of interest
- you have tried to arrange the project tasks to deliver what they want
- for reasons that you can explain, using the plans, you cannot meet their needs on this project

then this is almost as good as actually meeting their needs.

Stakeholder Management Actions

Once you have taken the trouble to produce this stakeholder analysis you obviously need to put it into action, so you must develop a list of extra tasks you will carry out (yes, they will probably fall into your lap for execution) to proactively manage your stakeholders. These actions must be real and positive, not woolly statements such as 'do not upset them'.

Typical actions might include:

- involving a stakeholder in some of the training associated with your project
- inviting a stakeholder to a demonstration of something working to specification
- inviting a stakeholder to take responsibility for something on the project, such as publicity
- discussing your risk management strategy with them, and asking for suggestions
- making sure you communicate with them, in ways which suit them.

As the project unfolds the stakeholder management plan should be reviewed at regular intervals, as some stakeholders will lose their importance, and some new ones will appear. This plan will form a vital piece of information for the project team, and for all future projects. As such it should be filed away at the end of the project, for future reference.

The Lake project stakeholder management plan might look like this:

Lake Project - Stakeholder Management Plan			
Stakeholder	**impact**	**attitude**	**action**
Sponsor	H	Worried about business	Let him handle Dorset Trust
Bodgitt & Duck	M	want more work	Display Board on Park House Gates
Herb Erriott	M	Reputation	Article in journal Interview on TV
Dorset Trust	H	Concern for wildlife	Show the plans

Figure SH02

Summary

You can forestall many problems with the human resources in and around your project by managing them in a proactive manner. You cannot leave their positive support for your project to chance; you must manage your stakeholders.

PKS Checklist

List all likely stakeholders	Even the unlikely ones
Assess their potential impact	Be realistic – not all stakeholders are High impact
Identify likely attitudes towards the project	Maybe ask them
Identify management actions	And build these into your plan
Replan the project	These stakeholder management tasks will cost someone (probably you) some effort, so keep your documentation up to date
Review and revise regularly throughout the project	You will not be able to see all the stakeholders at the outset

Part 3

Planning the Work

7

Planning with Milestones

Where are we?

You are at the start of planning. You have had your project definition signed off, and you are ready to start planning. We will look at project planning from the top down, starting with milestones.

What is a Milestone?

We must be careful with the term milestone, as it is in common use, with many meanings. In project management we will use the term with the specific formal meaning of 'a point in the project where something physical is produced'.

This simple definition is loaded with meaning in the project context. We will make great use of milestones in both project planning and project control.

The important part of the definition is 'something physical'. If your project produces a physical 'product' or 'deliverable' then you have an opportunity to examine it, and make a considered decision about real progress towards your overall objectives. If you can specify in advance what the acceptance criteria are for the deliverable then you should feel very comfortable when trying to measure the progress.

Some milestones (the ones really important to the sponsor) will be visible at the project definition stage. Major milestones are directly tied into what you are trying to produce on the project, and should be specified at project definition.

So, for the Lake Project, an obvious major milestone would be:
- *Pipe repaired to ISO1234, tested and signed off by Bert Simpson (the foreman from Bodgitt & Duck, the Drainage Engineers).*

This shows the full format of a formal milestone definition. It has the following parts:

- the milestone name, in noun/verb format
- the quality standard
- the testing method
- the person authorised to accept it.

Not every milestone needs such formality, but on every project there will be a few major milestones for which you would be well advised to develop such comprehensive descriptions.

You might be thinking how much work this might entail for yourself. Well, firstly, if you cannot specify in advance the acceptance criteria for one of your deliverables then you must either accept just any old rubbish that is produced or employ telepaths as project team members. Secondly, if you can specify the acceptance criteria in advance then the person carrying out the task will have a much better idea of what to produce. This means that you can start to build quality into your project right from the planning phase, by setting up a control structure that is based upon pre-defined quality acceptance criteria.

So, milestones are good things. They create a safe and secure control structure for the project. When you ask a team member how a task is going you may be told 'it is 90% complete'. You will have no idea what that means, but a milestone, however, cannot be 90% complete. It is either achieved or it is not. This makes for fewer arguments and a safer project.

When do we identify the milestones?

There are two ways of planning with milestones. If you are running a project where the pattern of milestones is well-known (and where you would be foolish to deviate from the 'standard' pattern) then you can indulge in 'top-down' planning.

This entails you identifying the milestones first, and adding in the detail later in the planning process. In any case, in most projects you will be able to see the major milestones associated with project deliverables, right from the outset.

The second method of planning is to carry out detailed planning first, and then add in the milestones later (bottom-up planning). In fact, many project plans are arrived at by a mixture of major milestones identified at the outset and then a series of 'minor' milestones added in by the project manager later.

Oh yes, you can add in your own milestones if you wish. Since they are an excellent method of keeping close control of the project there is nothing to stop you adding milestones into parts of the project for which you want closer control.

This leads on to an interesting suggestion. If you are running a project about which you know a great deal (you are familiar with the technical tasks in the project) do you really need a detailed plan (see the next chapter for some examples of detailed plan)? Maybe all you need is a milestone plan, which has less detail (and therefore will be easier to read and update) but which can be very safe in terms of control.

A milestone plan has a very simple format.

Figure MP01 is an example of a milestone plan for the Lake Project.

The Lake Project – Milestone Plan			
milestone	resp.	Target	status
M1 All equipment tested, on site	Bert	22/09	
M2 Lake fully drained	Bert	23/09	
M3 All fish in tank	Herb	23/09	
M4 Pipe tested to ISO1234	Bert	23/09	
M5 Lake refilled with fresh water	Herb	24/09	
M6 Completion Certificate Issued	P Mgr	25/09	

Figure MP01

This milestone plan is a simple list, and can be created using a word processor or a spreadsheet program. It has the huge advantage that, it being simple, the sponsor might read it, whereas he/she might not read a more complex schedule.

What happens at milestones?

Milestones are places where we (the project manager and the sponsor) can make serious decisions about the project, such as:

- All is well, let us go on to the next milestone.
- Things are slightly off track; make some adjustments to get back on track by the next milestone.
- Things have gone badly wrong; we need to stop and consider our options.
- Things have gone well so far, but we need to change the scope of the project.
- We need to change the budget, or the target end date, or the resources, and the technical solution, or the project manager, or the sponsor, or almost anything.
- We need to stop the project, either for a pause for review, or as a full cancellation.

To make sensible decisions the key players need facts and figures about the project and the actual progress. The project manager is the only person who can provide such information, and milestones are the mechanism. Examples of milestones being used to control the project are discussed in the Controlling Progress chapter.

Where do milestones come from?

You will certainly wish to consider:

- the project definition document (to identify the main deliverables and hence milestones)
- your own experience and knowledge of this type of project (less experience will mean more milestones for safety)
- your colleagues, team members, customers, sponsor, boss
- regulators or inspectors (people who have the power to sign-off something you will produce)
- books, manuals, guidelines, methodologies (which may explain how to break a project down into manageable pieces, each with an associated milestone).

Look for any deliverable that you will produce that can be used as a milestone checkpoint.

How are they documented?

Well, we saw in figure MP01 that a milestone plan could be just a simple list.

Figure MP02 is another way of presenting a list, this time in a slightly more graphic form:

The Lake Project – Milestone Plan		22	23	24	25
	milestone				
M1	All equipment tested, on site	◆			
M2	Lake fully drained		◆		
M3	All fish in tank		◆		
M4	Pipe tested to ISO1234		◆		
M5	Lake refilled with fresh water			◆	
M6	Completion Certificate Issued				◆
Figure MP02					

In many smaller projects the person responsible for every milestone will be you, the project manager, but it is worth thinking carefully. Can you find someone 'independent' who will sign off one or more of your deliverables?

During the planning of the project you should be able to estimate a target date for each milestone. Obviously this is easier with bottom-up planning, where you have the detail first and the milestones emerge from that.

By creating a milestone plan (even if this is accompanied by a detailed plan) you can keep the communication with the sponsor at a simple level. Many sponsors would be quite happy with a milestone plan if they knew that the detailed plan existed behind it.

Summary

Milestones provide not only the framework for planning the project but also an excellent control mechanism. Your milestone plan will become an effective communication and control tool for the sponsor.

For a smaller or more local project you may feel that a milestone plan is all you need for safe and simple planning and control.

PKS Checklist

Identify major milestones from the definition documents	Based upon the major deliverables
Add on lower level milestones to help you control the detail of the project	Based upon your own knowledge and experience of each part of the project
Identify someone neutral or independent who will sign off each milestone	And do not be tempted to sign them off yourself
As each milestone is signed off file the proof away in the project file	More of this in Controlling your Project later

---

8

Detailed Project Planning

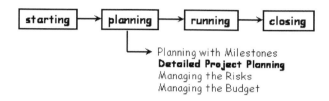

Where are we?

You've had your Project Definition approved, and maybe you've identified your milestones. However, what you want to do now is to start planning the project in some detail. Just how much detail is an interesting question, which we must answer right at the start.

What is a plan for?

A plan is a very useful document (or package of documents) for the project manager. Your plan should tell you:

- that the project is possible
- what has got to be done, in what sequence
- who will be involved, either doing the tasks or signing things off
- when things will be happening
- when things will be complete
- how the budget will be spent
- how and when you will be addressing quality, risk and stakeholder management issues.

So, from this list you can decide what documents you require, based upon the size of the project. Size can be defined in several ways, as follows:

Size	Meaning	Project Management Activities
Small	EITHER: Local to one department, running within the department's annual budget OR: Staff costs less than an agreed value OR: Duration less than 4 months OR: no significant business risk	• Project Sponsor, no steering committee • Project Definition • Milestone Plan • Task List (optional) • Risk Management Plan • Weekly Report • Sign-off at closure
Large	EITHER: Multi-site or multi-department OR: Budget > agreed level OR: Duration > 4 months OR: Significant risk to the business	• Project Steering Committee • Project Definition • Milestone Plan • Detailed Plan (Task List or Gantt Chart) • Risk Management Plan • Stakeholder Management Plan • Monthly Report to Committee
Common to all		• Consider Lessons Learned Review • Consider Issue and Change Management Process

What should your plan consist of?

We will now consider how to produce a plan for a more substantial project, on the assumption that if you can put together a Gantt Chart type of plan then you can easily draw up a task list plan. More properly we should use the term Project Schedule for the Task list and Gantt Chart formats, as these documents show the tasks, resources and timescales in one presentation.

Figure DP01 shows an extract of a Gantt Chart drawn using Microsoft Project, whereas Figure DP02 shows a Gantt Chart drawn using Microsoft Excel. MS Project is very powerful with many aspects of planning logic built in, but many people use Excel as it seems to provide closer control for the novice planner.

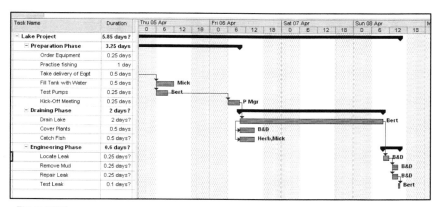

Figure DP01

69

task	resource							
Test Equipment	P Mgr	■						
Drain Lake	2 pumps	■■■■■■ ■■■■■■						
Catch Fish	Herb	■■■						
Cover Plants	Pat/Mick	■■■	■■■					
Locate Leak	B&D			■				
Repair Leak	B&D			■■■				
Test Repair	Bert				■			
Refill Lake	B&D				■■■■■■			
Uncover Plants	Pat/Mick			■				
Replace Fish	Herb				■			
Test Water	Herb					■		

Figure DP02

We will go through the steps required to produce a schedule in Gantt Chart format. You must decide if your own project is 'large' enough to need all these steps, or if you can be safe with a quicker, lighter approach.

The 6 Steps to produce a project Schedule

In essence these are the steps to produce a schedule for a simple project:

- Identify the tasks.
- Establish the ideal sequence.
- Estimate the size (and maybe cost).
- Assign resources (maybe not, if you are the only resource!).
- Draw the schedule (maybe a Gantt Chart, maybe a Task List).
- Optimise the schedule (make it fit reality).

Identify the Tasks

This task list should be as complete as possible, and should include all project tasks and all project management tasks (planning, measuring progress, reporting, holding meetings and so on). You will have the project definition to start with, but it may be worth asking some of your colleagues to get involved in this process.

This is one of the first project management activities we have encountered that fall into the category of being 'the sole responsibility of the project manager, but NOT a solo job'. This means that if you can get a few other 'brains' involved in the process you will get a much better result.

Ask your colleagues, but also consider asking your boss, your sponsor, someone who has no idea about the project (and who is not distracted by the assumptions you have made), suppliers (internal and external), specialists, potential resources, and so on.

Yes, this will make the process longer, but the result will be much better. You may have to listen to a lot of what seems like irrelevant piffle, but deep in the middle of it may be the killer facts that will make a difference to your success.

A good practical way of actually creating this task list will involve using Post-it notes, those universal yellow stickies, and a wall. The technique of drawing a Work Breakdown Structure (or WBS for short) is excellent for creating as complete a task list as you are likely to get. You can involve specialists, who can focus on their own area of expertise, and the diagram, as it emerges, will enable you to see the whole project in one place (as long as you have a big enough wall!).

Start by placing one Post-it at the top of the board or wall. This Post-it represents the entire project. Beneath that place Post-its that break the project down into its major components of scope. Take each component in turn, and break it down further. Keep on going, until for each task at the lowest level you feel confident that you:

- understand the task and how to carry it out
- can assign resources to it
- can estimate the duration and cost.

This means that for some areas of the project you may not need to go very far, whilst for others (maybe those areas which you feel unsure about) you may go further into the breakdown.

Figure DP03 shows an incomplete WBS for the Lake Project. Note that a WBS takes absolutely no account of sequence – this will come later.

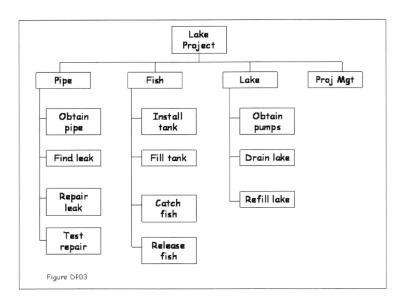

Figure DP03

You might feel that you wouldn't break the Lake Project down in this manner, but would use some other breakdown. That's OK; there is no single right way to create a WBS. If it is right for you, it is right. The power of a WBS lies in its ability to make sure you have a complete understanding of all the work required to deliver the project end product. It is a type of structured brainstorm. The diagram it produces is simply a step along the way towards our project schedule.

Establish the Ideal Sequence

If the project is small, local or low-risk you may be able to start the planning process at this step, missing out WBS; otherwise you must now sort the WBS Post-it notes into sequence.

So arrange all the tasks into the ideal sequence, with the minimum of risk (it may be necessary to take risks later, by overlapping tasks etc, but at this stage you should go for the ideal sequence). This technique produces what is called a precedence network or a precedence diagram, and example of which can be seen at Figure DP04.

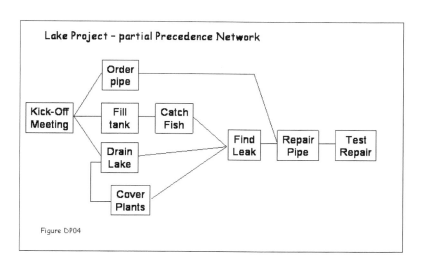

Figure DP04

By convention (and good sense) it is usual to have just one clear start and one end to a network. Not all tasks can be fixed into this logical sequence, as some of them may relate to specific calendar events (such as a steering committee meeting that can only happen on a certain date). For these tasks put them to one side – they can be inserted into the correct time position on the schedule later. NO account is taken of timings or resource availability at this stage (it is easier to identify resource considerations once this sequencing has been sorted out).

The precedence network diagram shows all the tasks and their ideal sequence of dependencies. Again you could use Post-it Notes and a wall. Once you are happy with the sequence it is a good idea to draw in the linking lines between tasks (but be careful that you don't damage the wall behind the Post-its). The linking lines will show problems such as danglers (tasks with no successors) and jumpers (tasks with no predecessors – they just seem to jump into life). You should have no danglers and no jumpers at all.

Estimate the size of each task (and maybe the cost)

You must be aware of the specific requirements for estimating each specific project. This means will you have to estimate and track the costs budget for the project. Every project manager must estimate and track the duration (some people use the term elapsed time) for each task, but the 'effort' required to carry out a task – measured in units such as person/days – drives the costs of the project. If you do not have to estimate and track resource costs then the job becomes much easier.

There are many common and practical ways of estimating the size of a task, as follows:

- Use records from previous projects. If you are lucky enough to have this information it can be useful, but must be treated with caution; are the conditions actually the same now as earlier?
- Try some of the work, and measure it. This may be invaluable for tasks that are completely unfamiliar to you, and which may be time critical.
- Ask the person who will carry out the task, but be careful with the answer you get. Some people are naturally optimistic and set themselves impossible targets, others will give you the answer they think you want to hear, others are naturally

74

pessimistic, others may be adding on some extra padding for their own comfort.

- Ask an expert. This may cost money, but may be worth it (think of this as a type of risk management).
- Ask the contractor. Again, be careful with the answer. He may be trying to win the job (and so the estimate may be light), or maybe he doesn't want the job (so the answer is heavy).
- Ask your colleagues. They may have experience of this work.
- Use a formula. Sometimes work can be reduced to a series of mathematical formulae. For example, if it takes 2 hours to paint three square metres, how many hours will be needed to paint 30 square metres?
- Read the manual. There may be some documentation that will give an indication of likely effort to carry out a standard task (very common in construction and engineering projects).
- Just guess. Nothing wrong with this if you realise that it is a guess, based upon some assumptions. Make sure you write the assumptions down (not to cover yourself, but to remind you to check them out once the project gets under way).

Let us remind ourselves of one dangerous problem with all of this estimating. It seems like good practise to go to the person who will be carrying out the task and ask them 'How long will this take?'

However, we must be careful to understand exactly what question we have just asked! There may be two possible questions and answers involved here:

- You may have asked – 'given a clear run at this task, with no interruptions, how many hours (or days) would you need to complete it?'
- Or you may have asked – 'how long will it take you to do this task?'

The differences may be startling. A very busy person, to whom you hope to delegate a task on your project, may answer '2 days'. Just what does this mean?

- Does it mean 2 days clear effort, but it will take me a week to fit it in?
- Or does it mean that I can do it in two days?

To be perfectly clear to your resource you may have to deliberately ask both questions, and try to establish both dimensions of the task in one go. The two dimensions, of course, are 'effort' and 'duration'.

Assign Resources to Tasks

Now consider the resources. You might not be able to identify actual named individuals, in which case you may have to plan for resource types (e.g. 3 Java Programmers, 2 Painters).

It is probably OK at this stage to plan for the most optimum resource availability, and to make adjustments later on when the schedule is produced.

There are two reasons for assigning named resources to tasks. The obvious one is so that you know who is going to carry out the task, but the second reason is to know how long the task will actually take (the duration). We might decide that a trainee, for example, will take longer to accomplish a 3-day task than an expert would.

Unfortunately the effort we have calculated earlier has little bearing on the duration. On many projects, where budget planning and control is not required, the project manager should be more concerned with duration, as this defines when the task (and eventually, the project) will be finished.

So duration is specified in days, weeks or months. The duration of any particular task will depend on a variety of factors, such as:

- how many people will be assigned to the task
- how much time each resource can devote to the task.

The relationship between 'effort' and 'duration' is usually not a simple mathematical one. Each task must be considered on its own merits, to know if assigning more resources will reduce the duration or simply raise the cost.

The standard management trick of throwing more people at a task in the forlorn hope that it will speed up the work does not usually work, especially if there is a degree of intellectual content in the task.

Here are a few examples from the Lake Project to illustrate the problem:

- *Catching the fish; well, if the fish catchers do not get in each other's way then maybe adding more people should have a corresponding shortening effect on the duration, up to a practical limit.*
- *A project kick-off meeting with all the team on site, on Friday lunchtime; it might just be that if more people go the meeting will actually take longer, not less time!*
- *A TV and Press Conference in London; actually the travelling time to London will be the governing factor in this type of task; if 2 people go then it will take one day on the schedule (the duration will be 1 day); however, if 5 people go the duration is still one day, but the costs will have gone up dramatically.*

Take the time to consider how much time each person will be able to give to your project. You may be using resources that have a full-time day job which they must maintain during your project. So, face up to reality; if someone says that they can only give you 5 hours per week it is better to discover that now during the planning, rather than later, during the execution.

By now you will know all the tasks, their relationships to each other, the resources assigned, the task durations, and, where appropriate, the effort and cost required for each one. You are now ready to draw the schedule.

Draw the Schedule

There are two main approaches to drawing the schedule, as discussed earlier. For a small, local, low-risk project a task list might be perfectly adequate, and figure DP05 shows a task list for the Lake Project, based upon the Milestone Plan.

The Lake Project – Detailed Plan				
	milestone	resp.	Target	status
T1	Order all equipment	Bert	15/09	
M1	All equipment tested, on site	Bert	22/09	
T2	Drain Lake	Bert	22/09	
T3	Cover Plants	Herb	22/09	
T4	Catch Fish	Herb	22/09	
M2	Lake fully drained	Bert	23/09	
M3	All fish in tank	Herb	23/09	
T5	Locate Leak	Bert	23/09	
T6	Repair Pipe	Bert	23/09	
T7	Test pipe	Bert	23/09	
M4	Pipe tested to ISO1234	Bert	23/09	

Figure DP05

You can see how the task list satisfies all the requirements of a 'project plan'. This type of plan can be hand-drawn, or created using MS Word, MS Excel, MS PowerPoint.

For a more complex project, or one with particular communication needs, you may decide that you need the sophistication of a Gantt Chart. Figure DP02 shows the Gantt Chart for the Lake Project.

Drawing a Gantt Chart is relatively simple. By now you have all the information you need; all you have to do is to decide on the timescale and time units for the scale along the top. You have no choice where to put most of the tasks, as the first one will start at the beginning; it is as long as it is long, and the next task will start immediately after it, unless you wish to introduce a gap.

You will probably not be able to draw the tasks in the Gantt Chart in exactly sequence you want, as it is difficult to represent tasks running in parallel on a flat sheet of paper. However, your precedence network diagram will show you the sequence, so many project managers will retain the precedence diagram to use alongside the Gantt Chart.

78

Referring back to DP02 you can see that the length of the bars drawn on the chart represents the durations of the tasks. There is also the example in DP02 of a non-human resource, in that '2 pumps' are specified as the resource required to 'drain the lake'.

Optimise the Schedule

These were the steps you have undertaken to produce your project plan:

- Identify the tasks.
- Establish the ideal sequence.
- Estimate the size (and maybe the cost).
- Assign resources.
- Draw the schedule (maybe a task list, maybe a Gantt Chart).
- Optimise the schedule (make the plan fit reality).

You have to carry out the first 5 steps in order to produce the schedule, but it is not until step 5 that you will be able to see if your plan actually works (for example, if it will deliver the goods within the published time constraints). So far you will have drawn the plan based upon the ideal circumstances, but now is the time to introduce reality.

There is a sequence to optimisation. If you undertake this in a random manner, slashing away at the plan, you may end up with the whole plan just unravelling into a mess. All your careful thinking about tasks, estimates, etc., could go to waste before the project even starts if you make a mess of optimisation.

So, the sequence is:

- Look at the resources; assign more, different (i.e. better suited to the task); allow non-critical activities to stretch.
- Challenge the basis of the estimates; maybe do some research (i.e. practise) to see if the estimates are reasonable.
- Change the sequence; take more risk by overlapping tasks which maybe ought to be done one after the other.

- Finally look at the task list itself; leave out some tasks, either forever or until a later phase. You may not have the authority to do this; consult the sponsor to identify low-priority tasks that the sponsor can afford to do without.

If this optimisation still does not solve the problems with your plan you will have to go back to the sponsor with some suggestions for reducing the agreed scope of the project or extending the end date. In all these cases, without the project plan you will not be able to justify your analysis and suggestions.

Contingency

It may be worth thinking about building in some contingency (sometimes called 'buffer') to allow for unexpected events. As you will see in the Chapter entitled 'Managing the Risks', you can deal with unexpected events by building in specific extra tasks aimed at reducing particular risks. However, there may be an opportunity right now to add in some extra time to allow for task overruns.

What you mustn't do is just add in a lump of extra time at the end of the project. This will draw attention to your lack of confidence in the project, and will be taken out with as little thought as you put into it in the first place.

Figure DP06 shows the Lake Project Gantt Chart, with two contingency entries.

1	task	resource
2	Test Equipment	P Mgr
3	Drain Lake	2 pumps
4	Catch Fish	Herb
5	contingency	P Mgr
6	Cover Plants	Pat/Mick
7	Locate Leak	B&D
8	contingency	P Mgr
9	Repair Leak	B&D
10	Test Repair	Bert
11	Refill Lake	B&D
12	Uncover Plants	Pat/Mick
13	Replace Fish	Herb
14	Test Water	Herb
15		

Figure DP06

80

Note the following:

- Not many tasks will need this type of contingency.
- The contingency is always assigned to the project manager, not the resource on the associated task (otherwise the resource will see the extra time allowance, and use it up).
- In some cases the contingency may cause subsequent tasks to be delayed (see 'locate leak', in Figure DP06).
- If a task takes longer than planned the resource must report to the project manager for help; you can then release some of your contingency to the offending task. In this way you can monitor the consumption of the contingency allowance.
- You should always maintain a contingency list, which details your thinking behind each allocation of contingency. At the very least this list will be useful when explaining to the sponsor why the project might take longer than originally thought.

Summary

Without a plan you will never be able to manage the project. You will be at the mercy of anyone who outranks you in the organisation. You will never be sure that the project will finish at all, let alone on time. Without a plan you have to worry about every task all the time; with a plan you will know which tasks are urgent for today, and which are scheduled for next week.

Planning takes time, but if you try to match the overheads with the size of the project you will gain all the benefits of planning without slowing your project down.

PKS Checklist

Decide on the type of schedule you need	A Task List or a full Gantt Chart
Plan your planning strategy	Can you get someone to help you in the planning?
Identify the tasks	The complete list of all the tasks you think you need; maybe create a Work Breakdown Structure
Sequence	The ideal sequence (you may have to overlap some tasks later); maybe create a Precedence Network Diagram
Estimate the size of each task	Task Effort is measured in 'person hours', or 'person days', and is a good indication of cost
Assign resources	Maybe not, if you are the only resource! Once you know the resources available you can estimate the duration for each task, measured in days or weeks of elapsed time.
Draw the schedule	Maybe a Gantt Chart, maybe a Task List
Optimise the schedule	Make the schedule fit reality, by allowing for all the various constraints that will be imposed upon your project

9

Managing the Risks

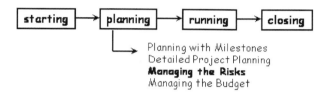

Where are we?

You now have a better idea of the work involved in the project, and you can begin to see where different people might contribute. You must now make your plan more robust, by introducing a healthy slice of reality into the project.

Just because you produce a document and write 'Project Plan' across the top doesn't mean that it will happen. Many factors both within and outside your control will conspire to mess up your carefully crafted plan.

Risk are things that MIGHT go wrong. You can improve the chances of the project happening the way you want by applying the principles of risk management.

'With any luck it will be OK', and 'How was I to know that that would happen?' are not professional project management attitudes.

Of course it is unreasonable to expect a project manager to be clairvoyant, but there are many so-called unforeseen project events that could and should have been foreseen.

Managing risk is not just about having contingency plans to help you survive problems.

Think about driving a car. Just because you are wearing a seat belt (the ultimate contingency plan) does not mean that you can drive like a lunatic. It is always better to avoid an accident by prudent driving style than to survive one. We all try to drive in such a way as to avoid accidents, but as we cannot control all the other lunatics on the road we wear our seat belt. However, we all hope to complete every journey without needing to use the belt in an accident.

We should approach our projects in the same two-pronged manner: what can we do to reduce the chances of something going wrong, and how could we survive it if it does actually happen?

The approach to managing risks here is very simple, but very powerful. It consists of several steps, helping you focus on the most important risks, and guiding you towards ways of managing them.

Where does risk come from?

Risk comes from:

- anything that is new; new technology, new processes, new people (project team, customers, support personnel), new methods
- anything that is unclear; unclear objectives or constraints, unclear technical solution, unclear resource availability
- anything that takes place away from the project manager's immediate sphere of influence and control.

Risk is magnified by distance away from the project manager (by the time the project manager gets to hear about a distant problem it may already be a full-blown crisis).

84

How can you identify risk on your project?

This is one of the project management processes that really improve if you can involve other people. Try to get half an hour or so from people such as:

- your colleagues
- people likely to be involved in the project
- your boss, the sponsor, the customer (if you think they can contribute in an open-minded manner)
- at least one person who knows nothing about the details of your project.

Make sure that they are familiar with your project documentation (the definition, and any draft plans you have produced so far).

A risk workshop in the form of a brainstorming session can be an effective forum for identifying risks. Don't edit what people say, and don't criticise or ridicule their offerings. Note down all suggestions, but make sure that what they say is specific and detailed.

For example, on the Lake Project, you may feel that 'Bad Weather' is a risk. Well, it is, but this is just not detailed enough to manage. Specific bad weather risks to the Lake include:

- *Continuous heavy rain during the pumping may delay the draining of the lake*
- *High winds during the covering of the plants with plastic sheeting may make the whole exercise impossible*
- *Sub-zero temperatures during the pumping may cause the pumps to fail*
- *And so on....*

Each of these risks needs to be managed in its own way, so must be specified separately.

Assessing the Risks

Once you have a complete list of risks you need to focus on the ones worth worrying about, and you can do this using a system of risk assessment.

It is based on the fact that every risk has only two characteristics that define its importance, namely the Probability of occurring and the Impact if it does occur.

Using a simple method of scoring of High, Medium and Low you can assess every risk, and then focus on the High Probability / High Impact risks. See figure R01.

The Lake – Risk Assessment		
Risk	prob	impact
Snowstorm during fish-catching	L	L
Leak difficult to locate	H	L
Pump breaks during use	H	H
Cannot catch the fish	M	H

Figure R01

Prevention is better than cure

The first thing you can do now is to focus on the probability of your chosen risks, and try to identify things you can do in the project that will reduce the probability from High down to something more acceptable (the equivalent of driving your car in such a way as to avoid the accident). These actions you will take are called risk prevention measures.

Prevention measures must be built into the plan, as they are measures that you will definitely carry out. They may have time, cost and resource implications, so need to be justified to senior management, customers and sponsors.

Some examples for the Lake might include:

86

Risk: Pump breaks during use

- *Prevention measures:*
    - *Ask to see service records for the specific pumps.*
    - *Make sure that the hire shop is qualified to deal with such pumps.*
    - *Make sure that the water filters are clean and fully operational.*
    - *Make sure that the pumps have oil and fuel of the correct grade.*

You should now add these prevention measures into your project plan, to make sure that you remember to do them, at the right time.

Unfortunately, you can do all of these things and the risk might still occur (it is unusual to find prevention measures that bring the risk to zero – you need another strategy to accomplish that).

Contingency Plans

So, just as in the driving example, where you buckle up your seat belt 'just in case', you need some contingency plans, 'just in case'.

You might hope that your contingency plans are a complete waste of your efforts, as you really wish to complete the project without needing them, but in some circumstances it might be worth actually testing a contingency plan in advance. If you have to fall back on it, and it doesn't work, then it is worse than useless, as its presence may have lulled people into a false sense of security.

You wouldn't usually clutter up your project plan with all the contingency activities (after all, you may never need them), but you may have to consider building in some research, practice and trigger activities.

Research activities are the activities you will carry out in advance, making sure the contingency plan is well founded. Practice is what it says, and triggers are activities in the main project plan which test the need to activate a particular contingency plan.

Triggers are often things you would have done anyway. For example, a test of a piece of equipment before committing to its installation, or a progress meeting with a key supplier to verify delivery dates; these are triggers if you have identified alternative courses of action (your contingency plans) and the meeting is the final decision point for activating them.

So, in the Lake project, contingency plans and triggers might be:

Risk: Pump breaks during use:
- *Contingency:*
  - *Arrange for another pump on standby (may cost more money)*
  - *Have a callout arrangement with an engineer*
  - *Buy lots of buckets and have the local Boy Scouts on standby*

- *Triggers:*
  - *Pumps fails completely*
  - *Pump runs at below rated speed*

Detecting the fact that the pump is running slower than its rated speed may require an hourly check throughout the night. This is also a trigger.

Organising these contingency plans and triggers may take up more of your time, so you must put these activities into the project plan (just to make sure you remember to carry them out).

Other Risk Management Strategies

There are other ways to manage risk, of varying effectiveness, as follows:

- Avoidance: just don't do the risky thing this way, or, indeed, don't do it at all.
- Transfer: get someone else to do it, someone who may understand the technicalities better than you. Of course, this

may reduce the technical risk, but it may also introduce higher control and communication risk.

- Insurance: a risk strategy , aimed at reducing the financial impact.
- Acceptance: some risks cannot be prevented (maybe you don't have the know-how, or the budget, or the resources to undertake effective preventive measures), or their probability cannot be reduced at all, so their probability must be accepted and you must focus on reducing the impact with contingency planning.

Documentation

It is most important that you write down the findings and suggestions coming out of your risk management, as you may have to justify extra project work to your boss, or the sponsor.

This risk register will be started at project initiation, and will be updated and reviewed all the way through the project. Finally it forms an essential input to the project closure and lessons learned activities.

There is a sample form at the back of this book, called PKS02 Risk Register. It is a suggested format for a simple risk register.

The Lake - Risk Log		
Risk:	Probability	Impact
Preventive Actions:		
Contingency Actions:		
Triggers:	Owner	Review Date

Figure R02

Ongoing Risk Management

The risk register will be a living document, and must be revisited at key stages throughout the life of the project. Some risks will fade away and others will appear, and you must assess and manage them all. At the very least you should spend 10 minutes each week reviewing the risk register.

Summary

Risk management can convert a theoretical plan into a practical plan, one which has a much better chance of delivering the end result. The processes of risk management force you to think critically about your project, and to use some creativity in deciding how to manage the risks. The documentation you produce will be very useful both during and after the project.

PKS Checklist

List all potential risks	Even the unlikely ones
Assess their probability of occurring	Use a simple scoring system
Assess their potential impact	Maybe on the entire project, maybe on time, cost, quality and benefits separately
Focus on high probability – high impact risks	These are the ones you must manage
Identify prevention measures	And build these into your plan
Identify contingency measures	And maybe build in research or practice tasks into the plan
Identify triggers	And build these into the plan
Document your risk plans	Possibly using the Risk Register example PKS02
Replan the project	These risk management tasks will cost someone (probably you) some effort, so keep your documentation up to date
Review and revise regularly throughout the project	You will not be able to see all the risks at the outset

$$\underline{\overline{10}}$$

Managing the Budget

Where are we?

You are well into project planning. You have produced your draft milestone plan and detailed project plan, and you have enhanced the plan by applying some risk management activities. You are now ready to calculate the project budget.

Do we really need to do this?

This is an excellent question to start with. Not every project needs to have a separate budget calculated and managed, as many smaller projects are run within the annual operating budget of the relevant department or team. In these circumstances maybe no project budget management is required.

In fact, there is a series of potential levels of budget management, as follows:

- The project will operate entirely within the annual budget, and no separate account needs to be taken about the project budget.

- You will need to estimate and manage the expenditure, but only on outside resources (outside your organisation), as this involved us spending real money.
- You will need to estimate and track all expenditure on capital items (things you will purchase during the project), as these may have tax, depreciation, grant and corporate accounting implications.
- You will need to estimate and track every last piece of money spent on this project, as we will charge the customer for the work, and we must make a profit (or, at least, not make a loss).
- You will need to estimate and track every last piece of money spent on this project, as the company standard is to have this level of financial control on all projects over, say, £50,000.

You must ask the project sponsor (and maybe your boss, and maybe the company expert – see below) for guidance on what you need to calculate, how you should present it, and how you should record and report it.

It is worth finding out who in your organisation is the expert in this sort of thing. You will not be the first person to calculate a project budget, and someone will already have established useful things, such as the standard daily cost of a full-time employee, and so on. This person may be the one who has to sort out any mess you make, so it may be as well to get them involved from the outset!

What does a budget look like?

It is usual to show the costs against the time period in which they are incurred, not when they are actually paid (which, in the case of outside suppliers may be several months later).

Project costs are often shown in the same scale and format as the project schedule, i.e. on a weekly or monthly chart. It is possible to draw the equivalent of a Gantt Chart or schedule that shows costs incurred as opposed to units of resource allocated to tasks. See figure MB01 for an example from the Lake project.

	The Lake Project – Initial Budget						
Code	item	16-Aug	actual	23-Aug	actual	30-Aug	actual
R1	Rental: pumps					720	
R2	Rental; tank					200	
P1	Purchases: Sheeting			450			
L1	Labour: Herb Erriott	200		400		1000	
L2	Labour: Bodgitt & Duck	100		600		1200	
R3	Rental; Dump Truck					200	
R3	Rental: Mobile Canteen					200	
M1	Misc: Refreshments					100	
P2	Purchases; New Pipe			150			
	Weekly Total	300		1600		3620	
	Variance						

Figure MB01

Many sponsors will not want to be bothered with every tiny detail (until things go wrong!), so it may be necessary to produce a summary for publication, as well as keeping detailed records for your own day-to-day management.

Figure MB02 shows a summary for the Lake project.

	The Lake Project – Summary Budget						
Code	category	16-Aug	actual	23-Aug	actual	30-Aug	actual
	Machinery Rental					1320	
	Purchases			600			
	Specialist Labour	300		1000		2200	
	Misc: Refreshments					100	
	Weekly Total	300		1600		3620	
	Variance						

Figure MB02

Where do the numbers come from?

Of course, how the budget is presented is all very well, but if the numbers are inaccurate then no amount of dressing up and fancy presentation will obscure this fact.

Actually most of the budget numbers come as a by-product of your detailed planning activity. The elements of a project budget are as follows:

- **labour costs** – and you can see this easily on your schedule, as you now know exactly who will be involved, and for how long.
- **purchases** – ditto, from the schedule.
- **rental** – ditto, from the schedule.
- **travel and subsistence** – this might need a little thought, but based upon the schedule you will be able to see where the work must be carried out, and you can calculate likely travel and subsistence costs, probably based upon your company standard rules.
- **project management activity** – this must be included, and will cover all your time to plan, monitor, replan and report, all risk and stakeholder management activities, and an allowance for team management time.
- **contingency allowances** – this may vary from one organisation to another. Some companies will want to see a contingency allowance, others will not. This is discussed in the Detailed Planning Chapter.

You can see that you have already identified all of these items as part of your detailed planning, hence the suggestion that a project budget is a by-product of other planning activity.

You will be able to use these budget figures to monitor the expenditure and report budget status to the sponsor. This control aspect is covered in the chapter 'Controlling Progress'.

Summary

Find out just what you need to estimate and track by asking your sponsor or boss. Also agree on the way in which you can summarise the information when reporting. Develop detailed weekly or monthly budget figures, and then summarise appropriately.

PKS Checklist

Discuss and agree the scope and level of detail you will have to keep	And find out the company standards for presentation formats
Extract the detail from your project schedule	Again, using company standard costs for daily labour rates, etc.
Summarise into appropriate categories	And use this summary for all reporting to the sponsor

Part 4

Running the Project

Starting the Tasks

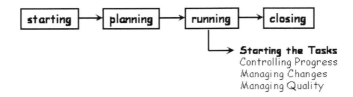

Where are we?

We have finished the planning process, and are ready to start the project. We now need to get the tasks started on time, by the person to whom the task was assigned. It is best to remember project management law number 2 at this stage.

Project Management Law number 2: Nobody on the project will do what you expect them to do...

Just as Law Number 1 (The sponsor knows nothing) sounded rather rude, but was actually an excellent guide as to how to approach the Project Definition Phase, Law number 2 guides us in the phase Running the Project.

Just because you have produced a project schedule and sent a copy to all concerned does not guarantee that:

- anyone will read the plan – they are busy people, remember.

98

- everyone will understand it – you may be using people on the project who have little or no understanding of projects, plans and so on.
- the key players will identify their tasks in the plan and diarise them as future reminders

Don't worry; your team members are not evil or lazy, but they are probably not full-time on your project either. They will almost certainly have a regular day job to carry out, and your project will be an extra 'opportunity' thrown on the top of what may be already a 110% working day.

Something will have to give, and as their day job is probably worth more to them in terms of performance appraisal points than your project, you cannot blame them for adjusting their priorities accordingly.

And those are the people who actually thought about it – many of · your team members will not get that far!

So Law Number 2 is telling us not to assume that your project team members will automatically follow the plan. You cannot leave it to chance, or their 'professionalism', or their loyalty to you. You must guide and manage the situation, and you can do it in such a supportive way that the team members will think you are positively looking after their interests.

In order for this part of the process to work you must have a detailed plan. Whether it is a simple task list or a slightly more complex Gantt Chart doesn't matter. As long as your plan tells you when each task is due to start, and who has been assigned to it, you can run a simple 'Work Authorisation' process. It may sound grand, but it is quite simple to do. It may save your project from the team member who forgets to start a key task on the correct day.

Work Authorisation System

Imagine a timeline for your project, as shown in Figure ST01. Imagine that Day T is the day when you want a specific task to be started by Jim.

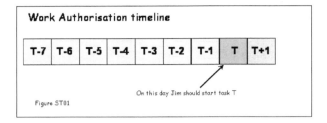

You must not assume that Jim will start on time. Remember, the plan may have been drawn up several weeks or months ago – he may just have forgotten all about your project in the daily bustle of his proper job. If you do leave it then you will not find out that there has been a problem until day T+3 or T+5 or whenever the task is supposed to be finished – it's too late to help.

So you need to have three conversations with Jim, preferably face-to-face, but via the telephone if necessary. An email does NOT suffice in this process, as you need to detect feelings and concerns about the task.

Phone call 1 happens on Day T-7 (i.e. 1 week before the task is supposed to start). You say

- Hi Jim – as you may remember in one week's time you are going to start Task T for me on my project; is there any more information or guidance you need from me?
- Is there any help I can get you before the task starts?
- Since we last spoke has anything happened that may have affected your availability for this task?

Probably Jim had forgotten the task, so you are gently reminding him about it. You sound very supportive, so he does not feel that you are hounding him.

The most important part of the conversation is the last part about anything that may have affected his availability. This is your opportunity to find out if, say, his boss has completely changed Jim's

100

priorities such that there is no time left for your task. If there is such a problem then the earlier you find out about it the better – you may be able to manage your way around the problem.

Phone call 2 happens on Day T-2, and it is an exact repeat of Phone Call 1. However, now that Jim has had your T-7 reminder, he may have started to think about the task, and you may get some useful answers to the first two questions. You can jump in with help, information or whatever Jim needs. Again, the third part is most important.

Phone call 3 happens on Day T+1. Actually some project managers do it on Day T, but I think we should give Jim some space to organise himself, and stay off his back until we really have a problem.

In Phone call 3 you ask some simple, non-pushy questions:

- Jim, did you manage to make a start on task T?
- Is it turning out the way you thought?
- Is there anything you need from me to help you with it?

None of these questions is concerned with hard-nosed progress-checking. We cover that in the next chapter. All we are trying to do is make sure that tasks actually start on their designated day, or that we pick up potential problems early enough that we can deal with them.

Summary

Project Management Law number 2: Nobody on the project will do what you expect them to do...

Don't get caught out assuming that your dedicated professional team members will even read the plan, let alone follow it in any detail. They are busy people, and they need to be reminded about your project. The system is simple, but very effective.

PKS Checklist

Create a diary system for yourself, based upon your project schedule	And plan 3 conversations for every task
Make your conversations supportive and non-pushy	But the team members will be aware of the nature of the call
Always try to verify the availability of team members	This is one of the principal reasons why projects run behind schedule

$$\frac{12}{}$$

Controlling Progress

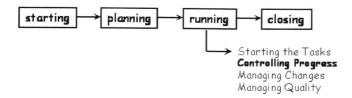

Where are we?

Well, work has started on the project, and you need to know if the project is running to plan (time, cost and quality), and you may also have to take corrective action and report the status of the project.

The principles here are simple, and are based upon the acronym FACE UP (i.e. we should be trying to face up to reality):

- F - Facts about progress
- A – Assurance about quality
- C – Confirmation of costs
- E – Early warning of potential problems

- U – Update the Plan
- P – Publish the plan

When should we do this?

It is not necessary to be absolutely on top of every task all the time. The Project Definition may indicate formal reporting times, and if so, these will be your opportunities to measure genuine progress before you write your progress report.

If there is no agreement with your sponsor or boss as to the frequency of progress reporting then you should find out quite quickly just what people are expecting. In any case you may prefer to set aside an hour every week to keep your paperwork up to date (project plan, issue log, risk log, etc.). Then when you come to write a formal monthly report, say, it will not take too long to find all the data.

Getting facts about progress

The usual way to find out what is going on in terms of project progress is to ask the people carrying out the tasks. The common method is to use that well-known approach, the 'How's it going?' question.

This is just not good enough, as you will have little idea just what the answer means to you. Trying to measure the progress of a task that is not yet complete is fraught with pitfalls. The person assigned the task might not understand the true nature of the question, and give you an answer based more on their consumption of elapsed time rather than their progress through the task (if someone says 'it is 50% complete' this could mean that 50% of the allotted time has elapsed – but I've only done 20% of the task).

The only way to be sure of exactly what has happened is through milestones. Everything else relies on guesswork, usually by other people.

Let us remind ourselves what a milestone looks like: the full format of a formal milestone definition has the following parts:

- the milestone name, in noun/verb format
- the quality standard
- the testing method
- the person authorised to accept it.

So, during the planning phase of the project you created a control framework, but specifying milestones at key points throughout your project. It might be a good idea to make sure that each formal reporting point is accompanied by a milestone. This will give you the ability to measure exactly where you are, and so your progress report will be factual and reliable (you won't be relying on the 50% complete nonsense).

Figure CP01 shows the Lake case study milestone plan updated with a really simple notation:

The Lake Project – Milestone Plan				
	milestone	resp.	Target	status
M1	All equipment tested, on site	Bert	22/09	OK
M2	Lake fully drained	Bert	23/09	OK
M3	All fish in tank	Herb	23/09	OK
M4	Pipe tested to ISO1234	Bert	23/09	
M5	Lake refilled with fresh water	Herb	24/09	
M6	Completion Certificate Issued	P Mgr	25/09	

Figure CP01

Don't forget that each milestone produces a deliverable that is signed off by an authorised person (ideally an independent person, i.e. not the project manager). You must collect and file each of these milestone documents as ongoing evidence of genuine progress.

So, for the Lake Project, a major milestone identified at Project Definition was:

- *Pipe repaired to ISO1234, tested and signed off by Bert Simpson (the foreman from Bodgitt & Duck, the Drainage Engineers).*

If you have the certificate in your hand, signed off by Bert, you know exactly where you are on the project. If you don't have the certificate, you don't know exactly where you are on the project. In the latter case you must now do some detailed investigation, going through with Bert all the tasks leading up to the milestone, looking for the problem.

Assurance about Quality

Well, this will come automatically if you rely on milestones for your control mechanism. Milestones specified in advance, with testing and acceptance criteria, will give you the assurance that not only are tasks being completed but the output from each piece of work has been accepted.

Confirmation of Costs

If you are running a project that requires budgetary control and reporting then now is the time to measure and report. Not all projects need this level of financial management. For example, a project run within the confines of your own department, with no external resource costs, may not need to be tracked in terms of its budget, as the costs are accounted for in the annual operating cost of the department.

It is worth keeping any allowed tolerance in mind here, as your project may not be exactly on budget, but it might not matter if the over-run is within the agreed tolerance.

Once you have agreed with the sponsor what types of expenditure you must track (see the Chapter on Managing the Budget), all you need to do is record the consumption of the budget as you spend it. Note 'as you spend it'. Usually this is taken to mean 'as you start each task that involves a budgeted cost', not when the money actually goes out of your organisation's bank account.

In most cases you will have no idea when your project bills are actually paid, but the act of starting a task commits the organisation to the expenditure, so this is a perfectly valid way of tracking expenditure.

Many organisations have computer systems in place that tell you (probably on a monthly basis) how much money has been spent on your project. These systems are notoriously inaccurate, and the information can be weeks out of date, so many project managers keep their own simple records of expenditure, based upon the assumption that work started is counted as money spent. It is often easier to track and analyse over- and under-spends due to project factors such as poor estimating if you are doing it yourself.

Most project sponsors will not want to see the detail of the budget, but will be happy with a summary. You, of course, must keep all the detail in order to control the project and produce the summary report.

Figure CP02 shows a budget report for the Lake Project as at 23rd August. The sponsor can see that week commencing 23rd August over spent by £150. This report could also be summarised by the categories of expense, which may be easier for the sponsor to read.

Code	item	16-Aug	actual	23-Aug	actual	30-Aug	actual
R1	Rental: pumps					720	
R2	Rental; tank					200	
P1	Purchases: Sheeting			450	550		
L1	Labour: Herb Erriott	200	200	400	400	1000	
L2	Labour: Bodgitt & Duck	100	100	600	600	1200	
R3	Rental; Dump Truck					200	
R3	Rental: Mobile Canteen					200	
M1	Misc: Refreshments					100	
P2	Purchases; New Pipe			150	200		
	Weekly Total	300	300	1600	1750	3620	
	Variance		0		150		

The Lake Project – Budget Report 23rd August

Figure CP02

It is worth spending a few moments at this point considering what your responsibilities might be if you are using outside suppliers, consultants, etc., as part of your project team.

Once a contracted resource has either finished or reached an agreed intermediate invoicing point he/she will submit an invoice for the work done, or the goods supplied. The invoice will come to you, as you will be the only person who can say whether the project has received the correct value of goods or services. Your responsibility therefore is to check and approve the invoice for payment. It is most important that you keep a record of each invoice as you approve it, either by keeping a photocopy or making a diary entry somewhere (maybe in the project plan) to record what you have done.

You will then pass the invoice into your organisation's accounts payable system for (eventual) payment.

The supplier will contact you if he/she feels that there is a delay in receiving the money for the work performed, as you were the one who commissioned it. Unfortunately you will have no idea if the money has actually moved from your organisation's bank account to the bank of the supplier, but you must be able to prove quite quickly that you did indeed approve the invoice for payment, together with the date of approval.

Your next responsibility is to find who in the organisation handles accounts such as these, and put the supplier in direct touch with the Accounts Payable person. Both parties will want you to get out of the way, as a project manager acting as an amateur accounts clerk will only mess things up for all concerned.

So, keep a record of every invoice as you approve it.

Early warning of potential problems

Most sponsors like to feel that you are looking ahead, and one sure way to demonstrate that is to include in your progress report a brief analysis of risks and issues identified in the last period. This will only be a simple text report, listing the latest 'nasties', and, more importantly, your action plans for dealing with them.

So, the input to this part of the control process will come from two areas:

- things which you have identified as potential problems as part of the 'getting facts about progress' activity above – these may be task overruns in time or budget, quality failures, resource problems and so on.
- things about your project which other people have reported to you – these are often referred to as issues, although the term really applies to your own issues as well.

Managing Issues

You need to encourage people to report issues about your project. An issue is anything that anyone wants to report about the project. At the very least an issue shows that there is somebody out there taking some interest in your project. Issues are good things, even if they may seem totally stupid and time-wasting. By handling dumb issues well (positively and constructively) you may encourage that person to report the next issue they encounter, which could just be a real show-stopper as far as your project is concerned!

Issues can be:

- simple misunderstandings – someone hasn't read your Project Definition, or is not aware of the scope of the project.
- early warning of a risk – 'have you heard…' This type of issue can be very useful to you in keeping your risk management activity up to date.
- a bug report – someone has found something wrong in one of your project deliverables; they are reporting that your product is not up to specification.
- a request for change – an issue may be the way in which someone reports that the specification itself needs to change; you may have to 'convert' this issue into a formal Change Request.
- a project management issue – the sponsor may be reporting that the budget has been cut by 50%, or a key resource has just gone sick.

You can see that each of these issue types needs to be dealt with in its own way, but a common feature of them all is that it can be very useful to record all issues in one issue log (just a simple list, with author, date and status). A simple analysis of the log may find, for example, that you are getting many issues from the same group of people, and this could indicate a training need, or a poor distribution list on a key document. This analysis will provide feedback on your success in communicating project information effectively.

Issues that turn into potential risks should be dealt with as new risks, as described in the Chapter Managing the Risks.

Figure CP03 shows a simple issue log.

The Lake Project - Issue Log			
issue	author	date	status
Pumps need special fuel	Bert	20/09	ordered fuel
Mick called for Jury Service	Mick	20/09	P Mgr to stand in
Heavy rain forecast	Bert	21/09	extra pump ordered
Local Radio will attend	Pat	21/09	Sponsor involved
Plant covers not available	Herb	22/09	alternative supply
Boy Scout camp on Saturday	Bert	22/09	Sponsor to liaise

Figure CP03

Updating the Plan

Well, you should have learned a lot from your examination of milestones, tracking the budget, and dealing with issues. You should have learned two types of things:

- **Where are we today?** Which tasks have been completed satisfactorily, which are outstanding; how are the resources performing; how has the budget been consumed; is the quality of the work up to standard; what have you learned about the project.
- **What does it mean for the future?** If there is a problem today can you think ahead; will this problem have an effect later in the project.

It is all very well knowing that you are two weeks late today, but you must try to identify the potential future effect as well. Your assumptions list may help here. Perhaps you are late because one of your assumptions was incorrect (invalid). Does it have an effect later, because it is likely to be invalid there as well? You are allowed to be surprised by something unexpected, but not by the same thing three times.

If the project is ahead of schedule you need to think: Are you creating problems elsewhere by forcing the pace on this project? It's always nice to be ahead of the game, but it may be better overall to drop back to schedule.

The most common problem, of course, is that your project is running behind schedule in some way, either in time or in the fact that some work was completed incorrectly and has to be done again. If the delay falls outside the agreed level of tolerance then you must do something to correct it. It is probably better to discuss the situation with the sponsor and agree some corrective actions before you write your progress report; the report shouldn't come as a nasty surprise!

Don't forget to physically update your project plan. There are many ways of doing this:

- Write 'completed' (or something relevant) next to each task on your task list.
- Change the colour of tasks that are completed (especially powerful if you are using a spreadsheet plan).
- Draw a line through each completed task; and if a task is only 50% complete draw a line through 50% of the task!

Figure CP04 shows an example of the Lake Project plan updated with progress.

The Lake Project – Plan (section only)			
tasks	resp.	Target	status
Install pumps	B&D	22/09	OK
Test pumps	B&D	22/09	OK
Drain Lake	pumps	23/09	under way
Catch fish	Mick	23/09	complete
Cover plants	Pat	23/09	under way
Lake fully drained (m/s)	Bert	23/09	

Figure CP04

Corrective Actions

Typically your choice of corrective actions is limited to:

- Add more time; put the target date back.
- Overlap some of the tasks (sometimes called Fast-Tracking); this will involve taking some risks, but it may just shorten the project enough to keep you on the original schedule.
- Add more budget; spend more money to speed things up, usually by adding more resource (sometimes called Crashing the Schedule); this needs care – will adding more people actually speed things up?
- Juggle with the resources; reassign people to focus on the slipping tasks.
- Reduce the scope; don't so all the things you said you would do; create a phase 2 that will tidy up all the bits you need to leave out, or hand them over to someone else, or just don't do them.
- Reduce the quality; definitely last resort, but maybe you've drifted into a Rolls-Royce solution when a Mini would have done.

Try out various scenarios by creating several new versions of the project plan. Which course of action has the best effect with the least risk? Maybe this is the one you take to the sponsor.

What authority do you have?

Most project managers have very limited authority when it comes to action to correct a problem. You probably can't decide to leave out half of the work just to get the project finished on time; nor can you draft in another squad of resources to speed things up. Your responsibility is to identify effective corrective actions and then convince someone else (the sponsor, usually) to accept your recommendations. If the sponsor says yes, then you may have to re-baseline the project plan, as you will now be working on a new basis for the project.

The Progress Report

You now have all the information you need to write your progress report. Many organisations have a standard format for a progress report, but the content always comes down to the main items. Remember the acronym FACE, and make sure you have all the relevant information to hand. You can use FACE as the structure for a simple progress report, which may be all that your sponsor and/or boss requires.

Figure CP05 shows a simple progress report for the Lake project, using FACE as the structure.

```
The Lake Project - Progress Report - 23rd August

Overview:            •Project on Schedule; slightly over budget

Progress this week:  •Fish survey completed by Herb Erriott
                     •Pipe material sourced by Bert Simpson
                     •Fresh water supply confirmed
Sign-Offs:           •All material and equipment delivered to site,
                     tested and ready for use

Budget:              •Budget £1900, Actual £2150
                     •Plastic sheeting £550 instead of £450
                     (recent price rise in raw material)
                     •Pipe £200 instead of £150 (more pipe
                     bought as a risk measure)

Issues:              •Mick called for Jury Service (P Mgr to
                     replace Mick)

Figure CP05
```

Publishing the Plan

At last; you've updated the plan, and written a progress report. What are you going to do with them?

At the very least you should give a new version (yes, don't forget to update the version number on all the changed documents) to:

- the sponsor
- your boss
- all resources directly involved in the project
- the project managers of all your external dependencies.

And you should consider sending an updated plan to:

- line managers of resources you are using
- suppliers and subcontractors
- any regulatory people (who will be inspecting and approving things in your project).

A smart project manager would, of course, keep a record of who has which version of which document, so that any updated documents can be sent to the relevant people with the minimum of fuss.

Summary

The acronym FACE UP really does sum up the responsibility of the project manager when it comes to measuring progress, replanning and reporting. The more accurate the measurement of progress (based on milestones) the better chance the project manager has of interpreting the information in a useful manner.

Keeping an open mind about the reporting of issues will make sure that the project manager hears what is going on in a timely manner.

PKS Checklist

Collect accurate progress information	Based on milestones rather than tasks
Physically update the plan	Show progress, both good and bad
Collect and file the sign-offs	These will provide a record of the delivery of quality products during the project
Maintain a record of expenditure on the project	Assume that as each task starts the expenditure is incurred
Record all suppliers invoices passed for payment	And find out who handles these in your Accounts Payable department
Document and analyse all incoming issues	Deal with Risks using the Risk Mgt process; deal with Requests for Change using the Change process; deal with all issues sensitively
Write a progress report	Keep it simple; more than 1 page will not be read by most bosses/sponsors

Managing Changes

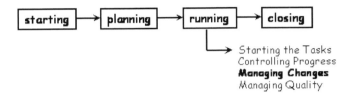

Starting the Tasks
Controlling Progress
Managing Changes
Managing Quality

Where are we?

Almost as soon as the project begins to take shape (during the planning as well as during the running) you may have to change it. The simple act of trying to write down a project plan will cause you to challenge some of the main characteristics of the project.

For example, you may feel that you cannot possibly fit in this extra piece of work that the sponsor has mentioned, as it is just too much to undertake within the timeframe. Once the project is running you will discover things that will force you to consider changing the project. Maybe a resource assigned to help you cannot do the work, or you are sick, or you suddenly see that the job is much bigger than you had thought earlier.

You will recognise the need for some changes yourself, but it is true to say that the sponsor will be the main source of requests for change.

This could give you a real problem, as the sponsor probably outranks you in the organisation, and you feel (and maybe the sponsor feels too) that what they say goes.

Now to some extent this is right, but many times the sponsor will not have any detailed understanding of the project (remember Project Management Law number 1), and so can feel free to make requests without taking feasibility, risk, budget, timescales and so on into account. The sponsor needs you to analyse the potential impact of any requests for change, and to come back with a sensible and constructive response.

So some of the facts of (project) life are:

- All projects are subject to requests for change (you can't stop the world just because you want to run a project).
- Requests for change are usually good things, as they show that someone out there knows that you exist, and they want to get the best out of your project.

All we need is a system for managing changes. With no system, however simple, you will be at the mercy of the person with the most stripes on their sleeve, and you will be dragged around as your project changes shape in an uncontrollable manner.

The Baseline

Managing changes starts at the project definition phase. The Project Definition, once agreed and signed-off by the sponsor and project manager, enters a special status known as 'baseline'. This means that although it can be changed every change must be agreed and signed off by the same people who signed off the original document. So, the 'project definition baseline' is established during project definition.

This baseline feeds into the change management process, as shown in Figure MC01.

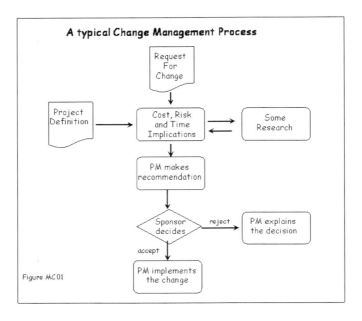

A typical Change Management Process

Figure MC01

Roles and Authority

In a large complex project certain key players will be delegated the authority to accept or reject requests for change, and this 'change board' may meet on a regular and frequent basis to keep the project rolling. On smaller projects the change authority will reside with the sponsor, never the project manager. You will not be able to change the contents of the project at your own discretion. The sponsor owns the business outcome, and therefore owns the right to decide about changes to it.

The role of the project manager is to inform and direct the decision-making process. This means that you will have to analyse the potential impact of the request for change, and make a recommendation to the sponsor about whether the change should be accepted or rejected (or sometimes deferred to a more convenient time).

The Process

Most textbook change management processes say that all requests for change must be submitted in writing by the person who wants the change. This is often a feeble attempt to cut down on the changes to a project, and is completely unrealistic. Not many junior project managers will be able to tell their Chief Exec to 'put it in writing or it doesn't get considered'!

The better way of stating this is that all requests for change must be written down before they can be analysed for impact on time, cost and risk. In the last resort this gives the project manager the leeway to write some of them down him or herself.

Many organisations have Change Request Forms, and these should be used wherever possible. Once you receive a change request you must:

- Make sure you understand it – send it back for more explanation if necessary.
- Start an entry in the change log.
- Compare the change to the existing baseline documentation (Project Definition, plans etc), and estimate the changes impact on Time, Cost and Risk.
- Document this analysis together with any assumptions and recommendations you make.
- Meet with the sponsor, explain the change and its implications, and make your recommendation for acceptance or rejection.
- Implement the sponsor's decision; this may mean
  - explaining to the originator why the request was rejected
  - for an accepted change, making relevant changes to documents, publishing the new versions of the documents to all concerned, and making the new documents the new baseline.

And, in essence, that's it. However, you may wish to consider a few small sophistications.

Tolerance

You may be able to create some room to manoeuvre in your project by agreeing some tolerance with the sponsor. This point was discussed in the Chapter entitled Project Definition, but it is worth repeating here. Sensible tolerance (for example, some time and budget tolerance) may allow you to recommend acceptance of some requests for change, as their impact is contained within an agreed tolerance.

Change Log

You may find it instructive to record all incoming requests for change in a simple list or spreadsheet. Obviously such a log will make sure that requests for change are not lost or forgotten, but you can also learn much from just reading the log on a regular basis. Figure MC02 shows a simple change log.

Change Request Log				
date	**author**	**change**	**status**	**comments**

Figure MC02

For example, you may find that you are receiving many requests from one group of stakeholders in your project. Maybe this is telling you that you missed them off a distribution list for a key project document.

In this way you may discover communication issues long before they become damaging to the success of the project.

You may also get some feedback about the quality of your own work. Many requests to change your design for a new office layout may indicate inadequate consultation on your part earlier in the project.

Note that the change log is simply that – a log. It may not contain the full details of the change, and it may not hold the details of the implications in terms of time, cost and risk. These details will be held in your working papers. You may wish to refer to these working papers in the change log entries, just to preserve a cross-reference between all the details of the request for change.

This change log will also be useful input to the lessons-learned review at the end of the project.

The Change Log for the Lake project is shown in Figure MC03.

The Lake Project - Change Request Log				
date	**author**	**change**	**status**	**comments**
14-09	Mick Brown	take Pat off night work	closed	agreed
14-09	Jerry Smith	can we refurbish the fountain in the lake?	open	waiting for OK from Sponsor
15-09	Herb Erriott	change of fish-catching technique	closed	rejected - too contentious

Figure MC03

Summary

Changes will occur. Publicise your change management system so that everyone can see that you are treating changes positively. Be fair with your estimates of potential impact, and always explain to the authors what happened to their requests. Feed the changes into the lessons-learned review.

PKS Checklist

Publicise your change management system at project definition stage	And agree a process for reviewing requests with your sponsor
Make time to understand every request for change before you analyse its impact	You can turn this into a positive stakeholder management activity, as it shows that you are taking care over such requests
Analyse the potential impact on Time, Cost and Risk	And maybe there could be a potential impact on the eventual achievement of business benefit
Make your recommendations to the sponsor	The sponsor owns the decision
Implement the sponsor's decision	Good communication with the originator is essential
Document your approved changes	Publish new baseline Project Definition, Project Schedule, Risk plan, etc., as appropriate

14

Managing Quality

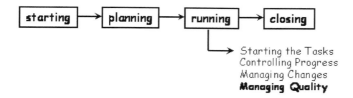

starting → planning → running → closing

→ Starting the Tasks
Controlling Progress
Managing Changes
Managing Quality

Where are we?

We are apparently deep into running the project, but as there are a couple of things in managing project quality that should be sorted out during project definition and planning we will return briefly to project planning.

The Quality Assurance Environment

The first thing that you need to consider during the definition phase is the Quality Assurance environment. Quality Assurance (QA) is created by building a management environment within which a quality project is almost guaranteed (it cannot be actually guaranteed, because we mess up this carefully built environment by putting human beings into the situation!).

The corporate project management environment should contain the following:

- methodologies, standards, guidelines, process maps – guidance for the project manager, to help project managers follow best practice
- templates, examples – templates and examples of forms that the project manager may wish to use
- project support – corporate facilities to help the project managers in areas such as risk management, stakeholder management, scheduling and so on
- training – coordinated training, with follow-up support to make sure that all project managers speak the same language and adopt the same philosophy
- software and systems – for planning, resource allocation, management of issues risks and changes, for communication and project control
- corporate data – to guide project managers when estimating new projects.

With the right management these corporate support facilities will not add to the overheads, but actually save project management costs. These facilities form the QA environment, and will increase the chances of every project delivering its business benefits.

If your organisation doesn't have all of these support facilities, do not despair – as long as you strive to create the Project Quality Plan then you may still have a quality project.

Quality Control

If QA is concerned with creating a management environment, then QC is concerned with making sure that the environment is working, and that the project is going to produce acceptable intermediate and end products (which in quality management is the term often used instead of 'deliverables').

It is too risky to wait until the end of the project to carry out the first check on the acceptability of the work. Even on a small project there will be opportunities to make sure that things are going well in terms of quality. Remember, from your customer/sponsor's point of view, getting the right thing slightly late is probably more desirable than getting the wrong thing on time.

The project quality plan (referred to as the QPlan) will contain a section where you can spell out the 'testing' methods you will use to make sure that things are being produced correctly, and this is described below, but here is a simple example of intermediate products.

For example, if your project is to carry out some research for your boss, and put the results into a short report so that the boss can take some action over, say, email security, don't wait until you publish the report to find out if it is what is required. There are at least two intermediate milestones in this project that you can use to get checks of quality, as follows:

- **Report Headings Approved.** Almost as soon as you start, draw up the structure (just the section headings) of what you intend to produce, and get the boss to approve it. The report should not contain any surprises in its structure, so get the structure approved at the outset.
- **Emerging Findings Approved.** As soon as you have collected your data, and analysed it, you can book a short meeting with the boss to approve your initial or emerging findings; it would be unfortunate if you completed a report but missed something that was vital to your boss, so get early approval of your work.
- **Final Report Published.** By this stage, the publication should be a triumph! Seriously, most of the surprises and misunderstandings will have been dealt with in a low-key manner.

There is obviously a strong echo of Milestone Planning here. Well, this is exactly where milestones pay their way. In the QPlan you can set out how and when you will get approval for your intermediate products.

The Project Quality Plan

This is not a plan in the meaning of a schedule, but is a collection of project management documents that, when added together, improve the chances of a specific project delivering its business benefits. Quality Planning is undertaken when the project schedule has been produced. This means that the project manager can now see the detail of how the project objectives and scope will be delivered, and all final and intermediate products (deliverables) have been identified.

There are four possible sections in the QPlan. They are all optional, as not every project needs all of the standard sections in the standard QPlan.

The sections are:

- Quality Targets
- Product Review Method
- Approaches to be Used
- Implementation Strategy.

The detailed project quality plan sections will include the following:

- **Quality Targets** must be identified in conjunction with the customer/user/sponsor. In fact it is the user/customer who owns the priorities and measurements that describe the quality targets. The quality targets can be divided into three main categories, namely Time, Cost and Quality (which, in this context, can be called Fitness for Purpose). The customer must prioritise between these three categories, and it should be realised that if one of these categories is squeezed then the other dimensions will be affected. Measures for Time and Cost can be defined fairly easily, but Quality needs more care. The measures for Fitness for Purpose can be defined using the acronym FURPS, as follows:
  - Functionality: what does the customer need the new service or facility to do for them? In what priority order?
  - Usability: how much work might the customer be willing to do to learn how to use the new facility? How much training is acceptable?

126

- Reliability: can the customer accept a period of breakdown of the new service? Does this vary in daily or weekly or monthly cycles? Are some parts of the new service more critical than others?
- Performance: how quickly must the new facility perform either in raw time terms or in terms of effort to accomplish a business transaction?
- Serviceability: how much will the customer be prepared to spend in keeping the new facility running? How often will maintenance be required? If it does break down how quickly must it be fixed? Will the customer wish to look after the maintenance themselves?

- The various dimensions of **Fitness for Purpose**, as defined by the customer, should have clear measures identified as part of their definition. The dimensions should also be prioritised, again by the customer.
- **Product Review Method.** This is the detailed description of how you will get your intermediate products approved. You can identify who will carry out your checks, when, and even how it will be done if there is a particular method to be used. For example, at one extreme you may have to call in an external testing authority to pass something as acceptable, or it may be as simple as a desk check by one of your colleagues.
- **Approaches to be used.** In this section the sponsor and project manager agree on the regulations, guidelines, standards and techniques that will be employed on this project (for example, Health and Safety Laws, Treasury Regulations, Union Agreements). If a company standard is not to be followed then this must be discussed, agreed and documented.
- **Implementation Strategy.** This section may not apply to every project. However, where this is a factor then the approach to implementation must be documented here. The reasons for strategies such as Parallel Runs or Pilot Implementations must be given, together with any extra costs or risks associated with such approaches. The effect of such strategies may have on the achievement of business benefits must also be spelt out here.

These QPlan activities may give rise to extra tasks to be incorporated into your project schedule, with their associated resources and costs. It would be foolish to identify extra tasks and then not carry them out because they were not in your schedule. Remember, some of your 'independent checkers' may have busy lives of their own, so you must plan in advance, and maintain their involvement in your project just like any other key resource.

The QPlan will provide proof to all interested parties that you are not driven solely by the time clock, but that you have taken due notice of the quality requirements of your customers.

Summary

If your project has particularly important requirements for a quality outcome then this must be defined at the outset, and an environment created within which it will be likely to be achieved.

If you are planning to have some of your intermediate products checked by a qualified person, then this checking should be identified at the outset, and built into the project schedule.

PKS Checklist

During Project Definition identify the corporate QA environment	Make sure you are fully aware of regulations, standards and so on which will affect your project
During Project Definition identify your project's specific Quality Management requirements	Identify targets and measures for quality, and agree them with the sponsor
During Project Planning make sure you incorporate the QPlan activities into the schedule	And make sure you inform and mobilise the key players
Review the efficacy of the QPlan at each project review point	And make sure that the quality checks are not unduly driven by the timeclock

Part 5

Closing the Project

$$\overline{\underline{15}}$$

Closing the Project

Closing the Project
Learning to Improve

Closing, not Completing!

There is a world of difference between closing a project and completing a project. It is quite possible to close a project even if it is not complete, i.e. you have not delivered everything you said you would.

Theoretically the project cannot be closed until you have delivered all of the agreed scope, and that is the standard way of closing a project. However, the sponsor or customer may feel that getting their hands on 80% of what they want right now is better than waiting to get the total 100%.

The key to closing a project (whether or not it is actually complete) lies in getting agreement between you and your sponsor that he/she is happy with the outcome. You stand a better chance of getting this agreement if:

- you have a clear project definition that describes what you were aiming at.
- you have managed the sponsor's expectations that maybe you will not be able to deliver everything by the delivery date, by focusing on the business benefits.

- you have a simple process in place that has captured any outstanding issues (so you all know what is left over).
- you have identified a way of dealing with the outstanding issues, and agreed this with all concerned (the sponsor and any users or customers that might be disappointed by not getting all that they had hoped for).

If the sponsor can see that nothing has been lost and that you will be clearing up the odds and ends then he/she may agree to close the project.

The advantages of closing the project are as follows:

- You have a clean start with any outstanding issues (new method of approach, maybe, to sort out the last few items).
- You can review the project, and start to improve your project management performance.
- And, most importantly, the sponsor can start to use whatever it is that you have delivered, and start to create some business benefit with it.

This final point may swing the argument with the sponsor.

Dealing with the outstanding issues

Of course, there are several ways of dealing with the outstanding issues:

- Make them into a new small project, with a simple definition; maybe you will be the project manager, maybe not.
- Clear them up piecemeal, under the heading of maintenance, or operational work.
- Just scrap them; don't ever do them; it may be that, on reflection after implementation, the sponsor realises that the main business benefits have been achieved, and the extra work required to finish off the last few items is not really justified.

In all cases you must discuss the options with the sponsor, and reach agreement as to the way forward. It may be that a mixture of all of these strategies is required.

The Project Team Members

Don't just let your project team members drift back to their day jobs without some sort of acknowledgement of their contribution to your project. This may range from a full-blown project party to something much simpler, but even if you feel that such an event will be inappropriate or outside the corporate budget then at least say thank-you to each team member.

It is also worth thanking their line managers for allocating them to your project. Remember, you may need to ask again for help, and you can ease that process by making sure you acknowledge the efforts and contributions this time. Some line managers may place a high value on having their team member assigned to your project. Maybe the team member will pick up new skills or knowledge that will be useful to the line manager. So at the end of the project ask each team member to document a 'record of achievement' for themselves. This is a simple list of:

- their duties on the project, and how well they performed them
- any new skills or knowledge they have picked up whilst working on the project
- any formal training they may have received on the project
- any training needs that have emerged as a result of working on the project.

Ask the team member to talk it through with you. Endorse the record, and send the team member back with something of value to themselves and to their line manager. This little job will not cost you very much personally, but might just help when you go to the line manager for help with your next project.

The Final Documentation

It is really important to get some written evidence that your sponsor and/or customer are satisfied with your project outcome. This is not just for your own personal glow of achievement (although you should revel in this while it lasts), but this final acceptance closes the file on what we all hope has been a successful project.

If some of the project work has been undertaken by resources outside your company then you need to get a written acceptance from someone internally to say that they are happy with your contracted resource's performance.

The sponsor should also share in this feeling of achievement (after all, your project may have been risky for the sponsor), so make sure that he/she knows that the project is closed, and ask for a signature on the Project Definition form.

Summary

Too many projects drag on because we get confused between closure and completion. It is much better to close a project and then start another clearly defined task to tidy up than to let the project run on seemingly forever.

A signed-off project definition closes the project lifecycle, and is an achievement worth celebrating.

PKS Checklist

Capture all sign-offs and file them	For all tasks where someone has accepted the quality of the output
Agree on a process for dealing with outstanding issues	Balance business benefits now against a 'perfect' project result in the future
Document and agree the team members' performance	Send each person back to their line manager with a record of their achievement on your project
Close the files	Store the project files in a central library of useful information, to make future projects easier to run
Celebrate success	And tell other people about it

16

Learning to Improve

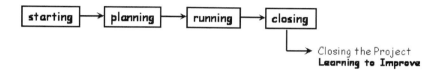

What exactly is this?

This is a very good question. We are talking here about a review of the way in which you managed the project; the usefulness (or otherwise) of the project management processes and documents, etc. We are not talking about any review of how well the business benefits are being achieved 6 months after your project has delivered (this type of review is the responsibility of the sponsor).

This review (sometimes called the 'lessons learned review') is carried out with the express purpose of improving future projects. You cannot change the one that has just ended, nor does a witch hunt or blame session help at all. This review should be structured and positive, and produce some constructive recommendations for making future projects more effective.

When does this happen?

Well, the obvious answer is 'at the end of the project', but there are other times when this kind of review can yield dividends:

- When you take over someone else's project. In these circumstances you need to establish exactly where the project is – this review structure is perfect.
- At a major phase end (on a long project). The whole point about a phase end is to take stock of what has happened, and feed that knowledge into the planning of the next part of the project – again, the review structure is perfect.
- At a major change of scope or objective. If the project is to undergo a major reshaping then a review to establish exactly where we are can be very useful – it will give a firm basis from which to move forward.

Ideally the review should be planned into the project, so that all of the resources are aware of it, the budget is allocated, and you actually carry it out instead of running on to the next interesting project without a backward glance.

Who should be involved?

Ideally the whole project team should take part in the review. This will include outside suppliers and so on. This gives the widest possible spread of input to the review process. If there are large numbers of people then you may need to give thought to the administration aspects such as having a separate scribe, a facilitator, white boards, etc.

Unfortunately, you may find that the cost of running a full team review is prohibitive, and you have to make do with just a few people. It is still worth doing, even under reduced circumstances, as some useful findings may emerge.

How is it done?

The format is that of a simple meeting. The project manager should run through a checklist of project management processes, and ask for constructive comments for improvements to those processes. By using a checklist the review can be kept positive (it must not turn into a personality-bashing session).

The checklist consists of 6 main sections, as follows

- Project Basis
  - Was the purpose of the project clearly defined, agreed and published in a timely manner? Did the project have a business objective? Were success criteria defined and published?
- Project Plans
  - Were plans actually produced and published? Were they at the appropriate level(s) of detail? Were they used? Were they realistic? Were time/cost/quality targets met?
- Control Structure
  - Were there appropriate levels of control? Were control procedures established and followed? Was the control overhead justified?
- Project Team
  - Was this sufficient in number, experience, knowledge and motivation? Were the levels of actual availability and productivity satisfactory? Did they deliver work on time, on budget and to the appropriate quality standard? Did they conduct themselves professionally on the project? Did the sponsor play a satisfactory role on the project?
- Working Methods
  - Were useful techniques and methods employed? Were appropriate tools used? Were the company standards and guidelines supportive of the project? Were the facilities and support satisfactory?
- Project Management
  - Did you have sufficient knowledge, time and tools to be effective? Did you have the right level of authority to make decisions?

Obviously the review becomes very valuable if the initial answer to one or more of these questions is 'no'. The follow-up question must be 'what effect, if any, did this failing have on the project?' From that analysis the project team must begin to put together some positive recommendations for improving the situation or eliminating the failing in future. It is these recommendations that form an essential input to personal and corporate improvements in performance.

Now What?

The review meeting should produce a lessons learned report, which will list your findings and recommendations. If the purpose of the review is to improve future projects this report should be used for two courses of action:

- Any urgent recommendations for change to the project management processes should be implemented and made known to your company's project management community.
- Any interesting suggestions or analysis should be made available to all project managers for their consideration during the project definition phases of their next projects.

These two actions may bring some practical problems. For example, how will you distribute your report? If your organisation has a central project support office then they should be very willing to help you spread this knowledge. Your colleagues (other project managers) should be encouraged to always start new projects by looking in the project management knowledge database, even if this amounts to a scruffy filing cabinet in a back office.

Ideally the report should be stored along with all your other project documents in a computer filestore, with a versatile search engine set up to handle queries. That's the ideal, but if you don't have such facilities don't despair; carry out the review and send your report to all your colleagues. This is second best, but better than nothing.

140

So, part of the Lessons Learned Report from the Lake project might look like this:

The Lake Project – Lessons Learned Report – 30th August

Overview:	•Project finished on Schedule; slightly over budget; all quality targets met
Project Basis:	•Very clear success criteria defined •Project definition easy to produce •Changes to scope incorporated easily
Project Plans:	•Two levels of plan produced and maintained throughout project •Plans used by all team members •Good input from contractors and experts during the planning process •Plans were very realistic, and flexible •Stakeholder planning was not wide enough, as we were caught out by the neighbours

Figure LI01

Summary

You and your organisation will never improve quickly enough unless you start to share knowledge about projects and project management. Keep the review short and focused, and make sure you document your analysis and recommendations. The wider you can distribute these findings the better.

PKS Checklist

Build the review into the project plan, so that everyone knows that it will take place	Plan to involve everyone in the project team
Make sure the review focuses on the project management processes	Use the checklist to make sure that personalities are not dragged into the review
Document the lessons learned in a constructive way	The only reason for doing this is to improve future projects, so your recommendations are absolutely essential
File the review report centrally, and tell people about it	Make sure that the recommendations are passed around

Part 6

Becoming Bolder

17

Managing Several Projects at Once

Where are we?

Well, we have now produced definition and planning documents for our projects. What we need to do is run the projects within the normal working environment, which will include:

- a number of packages of work clearly identified as 'projects'.
- a large number of bits and pieces of work, not clearly identified as anything.
- staff management work – recruitment, appraisals (both conducting and receiving), training planning, training delivery, informal coaching, counselling, discipline, writing procedures and guidelines.
- reviewing other people's work – either formally (in a Quality Review) or informally (just have a quick look at this, will you, before I send it out).
- company business – weekly/monthly management meetings, annual meetings, road shows, open days.
- company social – sports and social events, work experience schemes, sponsorship and charity events.
- social intercourse – just talking to people, getting coffee, going to the loo, fixing up a tennis match, buying someone's birthday present over the Internet.
- company administration – timesheets, progress reports, expenses, holiday requests, purchase orders.

- the Day Job – the project manager's 'own job', whatever this might be; projects are often assigned alongside a full-time day job, which must not be disturbed by the project.

So against this background of working life we have to introduce one or more projects. We may be really interested in the projects, and feel that we want to take them on, but if we don't do something about making some time for the projects then we will let people down.

How much time can you spare?

Project managers approach this question in a variety of ways:

- Ignore it; just go for it, and hope for the best.
- Be 'realistic'; you can always take some work home in order to catch up.
- Try to measure it; not difficult, but not very macho either!

Project managers are notorious for not knowing (or not wanting to know) exactly where their time goes. It may seem feeble and defeatist, but without some facts and figures about your workload you will never be able to manage yourself (and certainly never be able to challenge your workload with the boss).

So, how about keeping a personal timesheet for a couple of weeks? Analyse the results, and discuss it with the boss. It may be that your timesheet tells you that you are spending your time in exactly the way the boss wants. Conversely, you may find that your working patterns are not as expected, and don't leave any sensible time for taking on new projects. Just because you want to run a project doesn't mean that you will have the time to do it. The road to hell is paved with good intentions!

It is better for all parties if you can face up to reality in terms of your workload, and try to manage within it, rather than subscribe to the macho 'go for it' work ethic that often precedes a great deal of pain. If your personal baseline (the amount of work that you must carry out each day or week) is close to your feasible daily/weekly limit then this must be discussed with your boss before you take on any extra project assignments.

Another fact of life to face up to before you start to control this portfolio of work is the one of prioritisation. When projects come head to head with your day job it is usually the day job that has higher priority. Most bosses will feel that keeping the main engines running is more important than splashing on a new coat of paint. You might not like this (projects are often more exciting that the dull old routine), but it is vital to identify the relative priorities of all the elements of your portfolio.

Overall Principles

Managing a group of project alongside other work is more of a time management problem than anything else. The sequence to follow is:

- Write down all of the fixed activities that you must carry out (e.g. monthly management meetings, progress reporting to the sponsor, etc.).
- Write down all the staff management activities you must carry out and which you cannot delegate (appraisals, etc.).
- Write down all the milestones from your various project plans.
- Write down all the project tasks that are allocated to you.

What does such a plan look like?

Each individual project will have its own plan, even if this is nothing more than a milestone list. The overall consolidated plan, containing all of your assignments, will look more like a diary or wall-planner, as you will be trying to understand how all of your commitments fit into your working week. In fact a monthly wall-planning chart, photocopied and placed on your desk, makes an excellent working plan. Start the planning process by writing in pencil, as what may happen is that you identify changes that must be made to make the overall picture feasible.

Figure SP01 shows the basic monthly planner format.

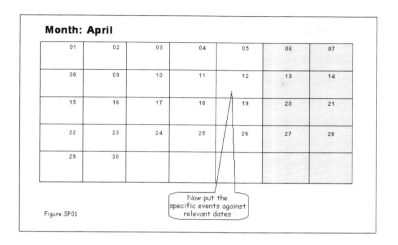

Figure SP01

You may prefer to use a filofax style of diary (as shown in Figure SP02), but in both cases the principle is that this type of multi-project control is actually a time-management issue using project plans as input.

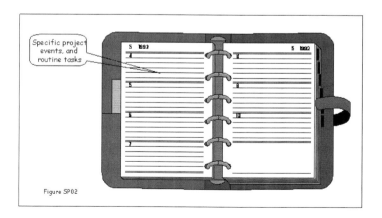

Figure SP02

Now you can analyse the situation

Look for the following:

- resource overloading, where, most probably, you will be the resource in question
- obvious clashes, with too many events happening on the same day – look for the less obvious ones, with undeclared but essential preparation or planning activity causing time problems
- portfolio risks – although each piece of work may be unrelated to the next, they all share a common resource (you), and so there may be dependencies between them; a problem on one piece of work may have a knock-on effect elsewhere that would have been difficult to spot without this type of consolidation.

What can you do about it?

In terms of resolving resource overloads the options are:

- Challenge your baseline. Is it right that you should be spending your time allocated in the manner indicated by your consolidated plan?
- Delegate. Once the overall picture emerges you will be able to identify those tasks which you can (and should) delegate.
- Defer. Put something off, until a later date. With the big picture and your portfolio risk assessment, you will be in a strong position to choose the most appropriate task to defer, as opposed to just putting off something and hoping that you can pick it up later.
- Delete. Consider whether you really need to do the task at all – a radical approach, but very satisfying.

The consolidated plan will change on a regular, rapid and repeated basis. Once you've drawn it you must keep it up to date, to reflect the movement of your own commitments. Many of the changes you wish to make will affect individual project plans, so make sure you reflect the changes at the detailed level as well.

Summary

Creating a consolidated personal plan needs a large degree of realism. You must start with the things you cannot avoid, and only put projects into any time that is left over.

Be aware that not all the time 'left over' is fully available for projects. You must leave some time for:

- routine administration that falls into your daily base workload
- emergency, unplanned or unforeseen activities
- new tasks delegates to you by your boss or your customer.

Part 7

Bigger Projects

18

And Now for the Big Time...

The PKS approach to managing projects is deliberately designed to be very light on things such as form-filling and complex techniques, but there may come a time when your 'small' project starts to grow into something that requires a more formal approach.

This chapter does not set out to be a full treatise on how to manage a large complex project but it will give you a few pointers towards the areas of your project that might need more attention as it starts to grow.

What other approaches are available?

There are several formal approaches roaming the project management world, with different characteristics and uses. The best known of these approaches are PRINCE2 and PMBoK.

PRINCE2 was developed by a committee commissioned by the UK Government. The methodology is very safe, but this comes at the price of bureaucracy. The methodology takes the form of a series of process maps, explaining what a project manager should do at key times on the project. In a deliberate attempt to stay flexible and non-prescriptive the methodology does not explain why the processes should be carried out, and offers no real guidance to the project manager on the detailed methods to be employed in the process. This leaves the project team focusing on keeping the paperwork straight, sometimes at the expense of genuine project management activity.

PMBoK was developed by the Project Management Institute (PMI), which is based in the USA but is a truly global professional body. The PMBoK (which stands for Project Management Body of Knowledge) sets out everything a project manager needs to know in order to run a project. However, the PMBoK is written as a series of expositions of key areas of knowledge (for example Risk Management, Cost Management), rather than as a process-mapped manual. This can make it very difficult to use as a guide during a project. However, it does explain the Why and How very well, which PRINCE2 does not do.

If only the two bodies would get together...

What characterises a project as 'large'?

Let us consider what makes a project so large or risky that PKS may not be sufficient as the management method. Here are some factors that might make you think about adopting a more formal approach to managing your project:

- the scope of the project – if the project is very large then you may need to have a broader project team; stakeholder management may play an important part.
- the technical challenge – you may need to start with a research phase, or recruit staff or subcontract specialists to work on the project; control of outside resources will require accurate plans and a careful approach to progress monitoring.
- the implementation challenge – the project may require careful handling when it comes to introducing its effects to the rest of the organisation; this may involve a wider project team, with specialists in training, HR issues and so on.
- the number of key players – if the sponsor is actually a board of interested senior managers you may need to sharpen up your reporting and communication activities; this will consume more of your time than the writing of simple progress reports, so this extra project management activity must be allowed for in the project schedule.
- the size of the project team – if the project team is large, or, worse still, split over several locations you may need more

formality in the planning and communication process; this
may include the use of planning tools to maintain and
distribute your project plans; it may be worth asking someone
in each distant location to take on the role of 'stage manager',
to look after the day-to-day issues at their location.

- the risk to the organisation if the project fails to deliver – you
  may need to develop fall-back activities, so that if some or all
  of your project runs into trouble the business can continue to
  function.

- the business requirements – if the business requirements are
  ill-defined or likely to change during the project you may need
  to beef up your issue management and change control
  processes.

Now all of these extra activities can be accomplished within PKS,
but your organisation may well have a guideline that says if a project
is greater than a certain figure (and this can be measured in budget,
duration, staff costs, financial risk or strategic importance to the
organisation) then a more formal methodology such as PRINCE2 or
PMBoK must be used.

Should I throw all the PKS forms away?

No. Fortunately PKS is completely upwards-compatible with both of
these well-known approaches. This means that everything you may
have already done in PKS terms will be of practical use in running
the project under PRINCE2 or PMBoK.

Should I stick to PKS?

I strongly believe that PKS, applied properly, will always be safer
and more effective than PRINCE2 or PMBoK applied 'by the book'.

In fact, both of these methods are very firm in their advice to their
users, stressing that these methods are so comprehensive that the
wise project manager will tune the method to fit the detailed

characteristics of the specific project. Unfortunately this is very difficult to carry out in practice, so many users of these methods follow the manual closely, making sure that they leave nothing out. This leads to unnecessary bureaucracy in the project, which, in turn, demoralises the project manager, the sponsor, and the project team members.

So, PKS can be used on projects great and small. If we are honest about it many projects run with no clear project definition, no project plan, and very little control and reporting activity. Even the back of an envelope will be more effective than that.

But then, I would say that, wouldn't I...

Appendices

Appendix 1
PKS Sample Forms

PKS01 Project Definition	Absolutely mandatory; your project does not exist without a Project Definition, preferably signed off by the sponsor. This is a two-page document, with the 'fixed' description of the project on the front page, and the progress information on the back.
PKS02 Project Risk Register	The realist in me says that this should be mandatory, as every project, by its very nature, is risky, and the project manager should identify and manage the risks proactively. The example here is a one-page form; obviously you may need several pages of risk register.
PKS03 Project Quality Plan	Optional; only required if your project has special requirements to do with Standards, Implementation and so on. The example here is a two-page form, but, depending on the characteristics of your project, you might not need to complete every section.

Please note: these forms are not covered by the copyright of this book. You are encouraged to copy them, change them and generally use them as suggestions for your own approach to managing projects.

PKS01 Project Definition

Project: Project Manager:

Objectives:	Constraints:
Scope: Included:	Scope: Excluded:
Roles and Responsibilities: Project Sponsor:	Project Manager:
Main Deliverables:	External Dependencies:

Milestones

Milestone	Responsible	Target date	Status

Approvals/Authorisations

Name	Approved to start	Approved to close
Project Sponsor		
Project Manager		

PKS02 Project Risk Register

Project: Project Manager:

Risk: Probability: Impact:

Prevention Measures:

Contingency Measures:

Triggers: Owner: Review:

Risk: Probability: Impact:

Prevention Measures:

Contingency Measures:

Triggers: Owner: Review:

PKS03 Project Quality Plan

Project: Project Manager:

Quality Targets: Prioritised targets against which the success of the project will be judged.

Approach to be used: Standards, Protocols to be followed; justification of deviations from standards.

Implementation Strategy: Outline of method of implementation.

Major Products to be reviewed

Product: Target Review Date:

Review Method: Reviewer:

Findings:

Product: Target Review Date:

Review Method: Reviewer:

Findings:

Appendix 2
PKS Process Maps

Starting	Project Definition	Getting agreement to WHAT it is we are trying to do, and WHY
	Roles and Responsibilities	Identifying the key players, and setting out their responsibilities
	Managing Stakeholders	Identifying the other players in the project, and what they want, and where they might be coming from.
Planning	Planning with Milestones	Establishing a structure or framework for the project, by identifying key decision points linked to the production of major deliverables
	Detailed Project Planning	Documenting the detail of who will do what, how and when
	Managing the Risks	Enhancing the robustness of the project plan, by planning to manage risks in a proactive manner
	Managing the Budget	Identifying where the money will be spent
Running	Starting the Tasks	Making sure that tasks actually start when you want them to start
	Controlling Progress	Measuring progress, taking corrective actions, reporting progress
	Managing Changes	Dealing with the inevitable requests for change in an orderly manner
	Managing Quality	Making sure that the project delivers quality end and component products
Closing	Closing the Project	Proving that the customer is happy with the end result, dealing with outstanding issues, and closing the files
	Learning to Improve	Taking a constructive look back at the way you managed the project, in order to get it better next time